THUGS, THIEVES, & OUTLAWS

THUGS THIEVES & OUTLAWS
ALBERTA CRIME STORIES

RYAN CORMIER

U OF R PRESS

Printed and bound in Canada at Friesens.
The text of this book is printed on 100% post-consumer
recycled paper with earth-friendly vegetable-based inks.

Cover and text design: Duncan Campbell, University of Regina Press.
Editor for the Press: David McLennan, University of Regina Press.
Copy editor: Anne James.
Cover photo: "Cowboy with Gun,"
© Thepalmer, Vetta Collection /iStockphoto.

Cataloguing in Publication (CIP) data available at the Library and
Archives Canada web site: www.collectionscanada.gc.ca

10   9   8   7   6   5   4   3   2   1

University of Regina Press, University of Regina
Regina, Saskatchewan, Canada, S4S 0A2
tel: (306) 585-4758 fax: (306) 585-4699
web: www.uofrpress.ca

We acknowledge the financial support of the Government of Canada through
the Canada Book Fund for our publishing activities, and the Creative
Industry Growth and Sustainability program which is made possible through
funding provided to the Saskatchewan Arts Board by the Government
of Saskatchewan through the Ministry of Parks, Culture and Sport.

CONTENTS

ACKNOWLEDGMENTS

To my family for their constant support, for reading all my stories, and for understanding that good people can be fascinated by gruesome things.

To Kasia, for her sharp eye and frank advice in editing, and for her patience and partnership in all other things.

To all the court clerks, journalists, authors, web editors, archives staff, librarians, and others who committed these events to the record, I thank you. The same goes for witnesses with sharp memories and the courage to come forward.

To all the bosses, editors, fellow reporters, and friends who read my writing and helped make it better.

Thank you to Brian Mlazgar (now retired), Donna Grant, David McLennan, and the University of Regina Press for the opportunity to write this book, as well as their support and encouragement.

AUTHOR'S NOTE

The stories in this collection were pieced together from various sources including court transcripts and other legal documents, newspaper articles, news broadcasts, parole board decisions, books, my own reporter's notes, and various periodicals. The source material was dissected, moved around, and stitched together in the recreations and stories of this book.

All the details and plot points are true. At times, people's thoughts are revealed through recollections and inferences later stated by themselves or witnesses. We can bridge some of the gaps and discrepancies in the historical record with reasonable interpretation, while others we cannot.

Where possible, these stories are based on facts accepted by an Alberta judge or jury as true. For the most part, they do not include alternate versions told by the accused or others. As is widely known, every crime has at least two sides. Only the official one is represented here.

Quotation marks are used when exact wording is known from records of the time. Quotation marks don't appear if the conversation is paraphrased.

These stories are focused on Alberta's crimes themselves. They do not extend to the years of emotional fallout that follow the families and victims involved. Likewise, there are many untold stories of rehabilitation, fresh starts, imprisonment, or continued criminality for those convicted of the crimes described in these pages. Those stories could fill volumes.

FORTY-FIVE HOURS

John Gamble handed a brown envelope to the first available teller at the Inglewood Credit Union. On the envelope, a mess of scrawled words explained he was there to rob the bank. She stared fearfully at him, with his dark, greasy nest of hair and stubbled chin. Across the lobby, his friend William Nichols stood nervously among the midafternoon customers. They'd spent three months in prison together and knew each other well.

The pair shouldn't have been in Calgary that March of 1976. Both of them had recently skipped bail in Vancouver. Twenty-three-year-old Gamble faced a murder charge for stabbing a man to death on Christmas Day. Nichols, a lean twenty-seven-year-old with a moustache and curly hair, faced an attempted murder charge for shooting a man in the eye with a pellet gun. Neither thought much of his chances of acquittal, and they decided to flee to Toronto.

The plan was to rob banks across Canada to finance the gas, drugs, and other necessities they'd need for the trip. They could lie low in Toronto once they arrived, perhaps with some cash left over. The Calgary bank was the first stop of the plan. Janice Gamble, John's wife, paced in the parking lot as a lookout. Tracie Perry, Nichols' teenage girlfriend, waited in the brown getaway car. She was new to the group, having met Nichols in Vancouver only a week before.

The two men carried handguns in their pockets, but neither drew inside the bank. It didn't have to be that kind of robbery.

The teller handed over $1,600 in cash while another employee hit the alarm. Gamble and Nichols sprinted out the front door and were back in the car in moments.

The four thought the crime was done. They still had forty-five hours to go.

* * *

Staff Sergeant Keith Harrison was on his way home in an unmarked car and plain clothes. After sixteen years with the Calgary Police Service, the forty-year-old was no longer in uniform since a promotion several weeks before. Harrison was a popular and well-known officer through the law classes he taught at Mount Royal College to new recruits and officers eager to learn. Some officers knew Harrison, with his square jaw and short dark hair, as the master first baseman of the Calgary Police Service baseball team. He was married with two teenage children. His younger daughter had died of leukaemia the year before.

Harrison was the closest officer to the Inglewood Credit Union when the holdup alarm came over the radio. In other circumstances, Harrison would've told other officers he would respond, but a broken radio only allowed him to hear the channels, not add his own voice. He reached the parking lot just as the robbers pulled away with Janice behind the wheel. The officer followed them unnoticed in his unmarked car. The two vehicles zagged through the Inglewood neighbourhood, cut through the grounds of the Calgary Zoo, and veered west on Memorial Drive.

Pull over, Nichols eventually told Janice. Let me drive.

Harrison caught up to the thieves as they pulled over on the side of Memorial Drive. He stepped out of his car with his revolver drawn.

"Drop your guns and put your hands in the air!"

Gamble and Nichols looked at each other in surprise. Their escape was spoiled. There could be no clean getaway while witnesses drove by every few seconds. The men, both armed, got out. They placed their guns and hands on the roof of the car as traffic sped by. Harrison walked closer.

"Get out!" the officer yelled at the women. "Get out!"

In the car, panic rose in the chest of twenty-year-old Janice. Her husband was about to be arrested. The whole reason they were on the run from British Columbia was for him to avoid prison. Yet, here he was, about to give himself up. She didn't want to lose him. With a scream, Janice leapt from the car with a gun in her hand. Her husband and Nichols went for their own guns.

A dozen rapid shots echoed across Memorial Drive. The back window of Gamble's car shattered over Tracie as she took cover on the car floor. Nichols emptied his .38 handgun at Harrison as fast as he could pull the trigger. Janice dropped her gun in the midst of the shootout, then tripped and stumbled to the roadside.

Only one shot found its target, a bullet from Nichols' pearl-handled Smith and Wesson handgun. The shot struck Harrison in the abdomen and pierced his aorta and liver as he tried to take cover behind his own vehicle.

Nichols jumped back into the front seat. Gamble scrambled through a shattered rear window and dragged his wife inside the car. Bloodied, Harrison crumpled to the pavement as the criminals sped away. Janice's dropped gun remained on the road not far away.

The plan was now completely screwed. They'd shot a cop. A road trip to Toronto would no longer take them far enough away. The women in the back seat were hysterical. They screamed and demanded to know what happened to the officer.

Gamble decided they needed to catch their collective breath. The group pulled into the Thunderbird Restaurant, a random choice in a city none of them knew well. The four of them waited inside until Nichols swore he saw workers call the police. The men pointed their guns at Thunderbird owners Laila and Ramin Kassam.

We just shot a cop, Gamble told the frightened married couple, and you'll do as you're told.

They returned to the parking lot with their hostages. Outside, the group realized they needed to abandon Gamble's car. The windows were shattered and the bullet holes along the side were plain to see. The entire group piled into a taxi instead. Laila Kassam was wedged against the driver, Doug Moran. After only a few blocks, Moran was suspicious.

"The woman beside me kept giving me a nudge and I knew something was wrong," Moran would later tell a friend. He hadn't heard about the robbery at the credit union.

He pulled into a gas station presumably to fill his tank, but instead headed for the station pay phone to call the police. Gamble followed him and pointed his nine millimetre at Moran.

"Let's go. I just shot a cop."

Moran refused.

Again, Gamble and Nichols abruptly changed plans. Gamble pointed his gun in the face of the nearest person behind the wheel of a car. Dianne Perry, a twenty-eight-year-old schoolteacher, looked down the barrel.

We just shot a cop, Gamble said again, and you'll do as you're told.

The group swerved through the streets of Calgary with seven people packed into the teacher's car. It wasn't long before police picked up their trail after they discovered the wounded Harrison and received Moran's phone call. The subtlety of Harrison's pursuit was gone, replaced by lights and sirens. The chase eventually led to the new neighbourhoods at the northeast edge of the city. Nichols knew they wouldn't last long on the open roads. He chose a home at random on 22nd Street and braked wildly onto the front lawn.

From her front step, eleven-year-old Tammy Ingram watched amazed as the car drove onto her lawn. She fled into the house as Gamble erupted from the vehicle with a hand around Dianne Perry's throat and his gun to her head. He screamed at police cars to back off as they pulled up to the home. Nichols kept his gun on the Kassams.

The seven piled into the Ingram house just as Elaine Ingram pushed her daughters, Tammy and Michelle, out the back door.

Nichols slammed the front door shut just over an hour after the bank robbery.

* * *

As Friday afternoon turned to evening, Gamble gave a pair of knives to his wife and Tracie with instructions to watch the hostages. Cut their throats if they get out of line, he told them.

He and Nichols tore the beds apart in the house and barricaded the doors and larger windows with mattresses and box springs. They pulled the curtains and turned out the lights.

Outside, police officers cordoned off the Pineridge neighbourhood. They fashioned a command post at one end of the street, as media swarmed at the other. A police helicopter hovered above. Ten tactical officers with sniper rifles, automatic weapons, and tear gas spread out around the neighbourhood.

At police headquarters downtown, negotiators discussed how to contact Nichols and Gamble.

Across Calgary, Staff Sergeant Keith Harrison died on the operating table after three hours of surgery.

* * *

Nichols spent Saturday's early morning hours on the phone in the Ingram kitchen. He freely spoke to police negotiators and answered all their questions. On the other end of the phone, experienced inspector Ernie Reimer ran the negotiation room. Reimer wanted to stall to calm the situation and to get to know the two gunmen. Before the sun rose, police were on a first-name basis with them. Several detectives and two psychiatrists were by Reimer's side. As Nichols requested, so was a reporter for the *Calgary Herald*.

Nichols was fatalistic about his chances.

"There is no way they are going to let us walk out of here," he told the reporter. "There are a lot of trigger-happy cops out there. They'll be ready to blow our brains out. I'll do it myself before I let that happen."

Nichols was nervous and talkative. He emphasized repeatedly that he and Gamble were not going back to jail. "We prefer death to going behind bars again. I would personally take a gun and stick it in my mouth and blow my head off before I will go back to jail."

Detective Doug Green took note of the suicidal talk. That wasn't how he wanted it to end. Even for cop killers, Canada was about to abolish executions.

"Remember, Bill," he told Nichols over the line, "there is no capital punishment now. And jail can't be that bad. You can apply for parole."

The first demand Nichols and Gamble made was simple. They wanted $100,000. In the middle of the night, police woke bank managers to collect the money from two Bank of Montreal locations. Giving the gang that much cash was a bad idea, Reimer knew, but he wanted it nearby in case it became necessary. For now, the cash would stay with him.

Around 3:30 a.m., the demands became more complicated. Nichols wanted painkillers, cigarettes, "the best damn lawyer in the city," and a promise that Janice and Tracie wouldn't be charged when it was over. They would simply walk away, Nichols demanded.

"They were not involved," he said. "Their only crime was to love us."

At headquarters, Reimer saw his chance. If police were going to supply cigarettes and drugs, negotiators told the gunmen, they needed to show good faith. They needed to send out a hostage. Nichols agreed.

In the dark, but still dreadfully exposed, a police officer approached the front of the home with a pack of cigarettes and Demerol, a painkiller. He threw the package onto the front step and dashed back to cover.

A few minutes later, Nichols phoned the negotiation room and claimed the vials of Demerol had smashed on the step. The drugs were useless and they wanted more, he said. Reimer and other officers didn't believe the story. They were all experienced enough to recognize drug-seeking behaviour. Still, they couldn't prove the lie, and a hostage was at stake. An officer crept across the lawn again and delivered another drug packet.

There was no phone call of complaint this time. Inside the house, the three hostages heard no talk about who might be released first. They were on the bedroom carpet in the dark, with Janice and Tracie on watch. The women with the knives were nice enough, Laila Kassam thought. They weren't like the men. Janice and Tracie hadn't hurt them and had even brought food and coffee for her husband, herself, and the young schoolteacher. Bizarre as it was, they were nice.

Shortly after, the gunmen sent Ramin Kassam out the front door unharmed.

For the rest of Saturday morning, police could hear the mood change in the house. Nichols and Gamble talked and laughed loudly as the Demerol took hold. In the night, the men told Janice they might surrender at sunrise. It had to be in daylight, they stressed, so police couldn't simply gun them down.

Police investigators had discovered more about Nichols and Gamble by the time the sun rose. They knew the pair had skipped bail on charges in Vancouver. Gamble's lawyer in Vancouver, Jim Hogan, was now on his way to Calgary in the hope he could negotiate with his client. Hogan had experience negotiating with hostage-takers in the British Columbia prison system. He'd been in three similar situations before.

No one came out of the house Saturday morning. The phone calls went back and forth in an attempt to get Hogan inside. Nichols and Gamble made more demands. They wanted Hogan to deliver a large amount of heroin and soda. The request for heroin set off a debate at police headquarters. They couldn't just send hard drugs in through the front door, but it was risky to refuse. The two men were drug addicts and would soon get desperate for a high. They decided to give the gunmen methadone, a synthetic drug used in the treatment of heroin addicts.

In the afternoon, the four bank robbers discussed the possibility of simply killing themselves. None of them could see a clean way out. The Gambles and Nichols agreed suicide was the best plan, but Tracie rejected it outright. Eventually, Janice changed her mind.

Saturday evening, Hogan walked through the front door with two cartons of pop and the methadone. Police snipers struggled to see inside with the curtains pulled. Inside, Hogan ensured the two hostages were alive, then talked to the gang over a round of Cokes.

Nichols and Gamble were willing to send out the last two hostages. The men were convinced they wouldn't leave the house alive, and the hostages were no longer useful. The two women the gunmen loved would also leave, it was agreed.

Hogan told the four that Nichols and the Gambles would be charged with Harrison's murder. Janice reversed her earlier decision and wanted to stay. Her husband insisted she leave.

Thirty-five minutes after Hogan walked inside, he came back out with hostages Laila Kassam and Dianne Perry. It was the first time Kassam believed she would survive.

Janice and Tracie left together. Nichols and Tracie hugged on the front step before he disappeared back inside. Crying, Janice tried to turn back as she reached the sidewalk. Tracie and Hogan grabbed her arms and forced her to walk away.

The front door shut again, and Gamble and Nichols were alone. The two men made a suicide pact. They would overdose on the methadone and leave the whole mess behind them, Gamble said. Nichols agreed, but then poured half his drugs down the kitchen sink behind Gamble's back.

They sat on the living room couch and shot up.

The police didn't hear anything from the house Sunday morning as they waited for the noon deadline set for them to surrender. Reimer phoned countless times. Officers on

.the street called to Nichols and Gamble through a bullhorn. Hogan walked up the driveway and pounded on the garage door. The noon deadline passed. The police couldn't wait any longer.

A tactical team of five officers stormed the house. They clouded the home with tear gas and went inside by the front and back doors. An excruciating silence fell until an officer's voice came over the radio.

"Pair down and out," he said. "One still breathing."

Gamble was dead of an overdose on the living room floor. Beside him, Nichols was unconscious and in critical condition. Both his and Gamble's guns were on the carpet near his outstretched hands.

Police were surprised. They'd expected a fight. No one believed such a chaotic forty-five hours would end so quietly.

On March 16, 1976, Staff Sergeant Keith Harrison was buried at a cemetery near Rosedale United Church. Police Chief Brian Sawyer gave the eulogy. Harrison's coffin, covered in roses and a Canadian flag, was carried by fellow police officers and his brother Gary. All officers in Calgary walking the beat held two minutes of silence wherever they happened to be when Harrison's service began. Harrison's honour guard was made up of twenty-two rookie officers who graduated the day he was killed.

William Nichols was in a bed at Calgary General Hospital for more than a month with severe kidney damage from the methadone.

In November 1976, Nichols and Janice were brought before a jury on murder charges. Gamble was represented by Hogan, her late husband's lawyer. Tracie was held by police as a crucial witness and was never charged.

Nichols and Janice Gamble were both convicted and given life sentences.

HEAVY METAL

For sixteen years, Narin Sok and Deang Huon deeply wanted a child. The Cambodian refugees lived a quiet, contented life in their small downtown Edmonton apartment. They had met by chance in a shopping mall when Sok recognized Huon's aunt from a Thai refugee camp, back when his life was focused on escape from violence and war. Sok was taken with her as soon as they were introduced and quickly asked a friend to arrange another meeting. They dated for several months and were married the next year.

They lived near the sprawling view of the North Saskatchewan River Valley, in the Kent Apartments, home to many other Cambodian families they called friends. He worked in a scrap-metal yard and she cleaned business offices in the evenings. The marriage was happy, Sok would later tell psychiatrists, with no violence and few arguments. Still, year after year, they failed to have the children both hoped for.

Sok was born into a large family in a tiny village in Cambodia in 1959, the ninth of a dozen children. As a teenager, he'd already lost four brothers and two sisters to disease or the violence that plagued the country. Eventually, he was forced into life as a child soldier and spent years in a civil war that marked him with shrapnel wounds and scars. Even when he returned to the family farm, he worked atop unexploded mines under the watch of the armed guards of the sadistic dictator Pol Pot.

At nineteen, he escaped to Thailand and six years later, in 1986, he left the Thai refugee camps and travelled to Edmonton. At work, he peeled plastic from wires and cables so the metal inside could be recycled. He was always the smallest worker in the yard, he recalled. He usually didn't wear the protective masks that made workers sweat in hot weather. The mask turned black on the outside from the airborne toxic dust on the rare occasions he did wear one.

In September of 2007, Sok visited his many relatives in Cambodia with the lack of his own children on his mind. He was already forty-nine and Huon was thirty-eight. Perhaps there was something else that might help, he thought. While in his home country for a month, Sok bought two fertility belts held together by chains and amulets of zinc, silver, and lead. Sok was told they were magic. He showed them to a monk he knew at the Cambodian Buddhist Temple in Edmonton when he arrived home.

"You should order two more of these belts," the monk told him.

Sok paid a thousand dollars each for the belts he was convinced would finally help him and Huon conceive. Each wore two of the belts at home and work to increase their chances of conceiving a child. However, as 2007 turned into 2008, the couple still was not pregnant.

At General Scrap Metals, Sok's co-workers noticed gradual changes in him once he returned from his last visit to Cambodia. He was known as a model employee, an obsessive man who worked hard and obeyed all the rules except for wearing his protective mask. He never missed work.

"I wish I could have ten workers like Narin Sok," said his supervisor, Marc Teepell.

In the first months of 2008, Teepell noticed Sok was irritable and obsessive. Everything needed to be in its proper place. He threw a fit when someone left muddy boots in front of his locker, something no one expected from the small, pleasant man. His best friend of twenty-six years, Dieng Thach, also noticed changes. Sok no longer wanted to talk about anything. He demanded changes to minor procedures such as how materials were sorted and which kind of pallets were used.

"Stop saying good morning to me," Sok told a fellow worker one day. "No one likes me."

His behaviour at home changed as well. Huon's cousin, Sina Chan, noticed a sudden weirdness in the couple's life. Sok hoarded huge, forty-pound bags of rice. He'd crammed twenty of them into the couple's small apartment.

In the third week of July 2008, Sok became convinced Huon's mother was ill at her home in the southern Alberta town of Brooks and needed their help. The couple drove as far south as Red Deer before their car broke down. Determined, Sok paid $700 dollars for a taxi to take them the rest of the way, through a third of the province. Once they arrived, they discovered Huon's mother was fine, as healthy as she'd been the week before. Luon Huon, Deang's brother, was surprised at the visit. He was even more surprised when Sok asked to speak to him apart from the others.

"There are two guys coming after me and they are going to kill me," Sok confided to his brother-in-law. "They are in a red car and it circled me many times. You don't believe me but there are people after me."

Sok was so adamant his brother-in-law took him to the Brooks RCMP detachment.

You have to report that in Edmonton, where it happened, they were told by an officer.

"I want to speak to someone in the government," Sok replied.

Luon Huon drove the couple back to Edmonton. He called his sister two days later, on July 29, to check up on them. Sok was still acting strangely, Deang Huon told her brother. Her husband sliced up black garbage bags and taped them over the windows. He moved furniture around haphazardly and no longer wanted anyone but himself and

Huon to enter the apartment. Unbeknownst to Huon, Sok told his boss he couldn't work because his wife was ill. He told Huon he stayed home because strange people followed him everywhere.

Chan visited the apartment the same day. Sok answered the door exhausted, bathed in sweat, with a knife clutched in his hand. Chan backed away down the apartment hall and called her cousin at work to discuss her husband. Huon said not to worry. Sok only carried the knife to cut garbage bags and hadn't threatened her. He'd never hurt her in sixteen years of marriage. No, Huon said, there was no reason to call police or have relatives stay at the apartment.

Chan was unconvinced. She called the apartment twenty times the next day before Sok answered and said Huon was asleep and couldn't come to the phone. Chan said she didn't believe him, and Sok hung up. Chan's next call was to the police.

That evening, police arrived at the Kent Apartments and told the landlord to unlock the apartment door after their knocks went unanswered. The door was barricaded with furniture and sacks of rice, and it took three officers to force their way through. Inside, the apartment was black because of the garbage bags over the windows, though a thin light shone under the door of the master bedroom. It reeked of some sort of foul smoke. Sok had disabled the smoke detector.

Again, officers shoved open a door barricaded with sacks of rice. Inside the couple's bedroom, Sok sat on the bed in the midst of more rice, torn garbage bags, and strewn clothing that covered the floor. Sok said nothing. Huon's leg stuck out from the mess on the floor, already stiff with rigor mortis.

In a holding cell at police headquarters, Sok spat on the walls, urinated on the floor, and demanded the phone number for the prime minister of Canada.

"I didn't kill my wife," he told officers in Cambodian. He was taken to the Royal Alexandra Hospital where doctors discovered toxic damage to his kidneys, liver, and heart.

Sok had killed his wife, but remembered nothing of it.

He didn't remember his attack on her, or the fight that left him with a black eye and scratches all over his body. He couldn't recall sticking a slim piece of metal through his wife's arm or why he'd done it. He had a vague memory of placing a chair astride his wife's neck and using a sack of rice to weigh it down. Perhaps his wife had been possessed by the "snake spirit" of his long-dead brother, he said to investigators hours after his arrest.

What he did recall was that he'd thrown the couple's four fertility belts into a pan on the stove and tried to melt them for hours before the couple fought. Their magic had never worked, never brought him a child. The toxic smoke from the combination of zinc, silver, and lead clouded in the small apartment, unable to vent because of the garbage bags taped over the windows.

Blood samples taken from Sok the night of his arrest showed toxic levels of lead, cadmium, and manganese. His body was flooded with metals. Doctors determined Sok's toxicity began with nine years of working without his mask at the scrap-metal yard and gradually caused paranoia and severe personality shifts. The cheaply made fertility belts he wore each day made his health worse. The poisoning reached its highest level when he burned the fertility belts out of frustration and inhaled the toxic smoke for hours.

At his murder trial, after months in a psychiatric hospital had finally allowed the toxic chemicals to leave his system, Sok was found not criminally responsible for the murder of his wife because of his rare mental illness. He sat still in the prisoner's box, hunched over in a standard blue jumpsuit, and looked at no one as he was cleared of a charge of second-degree murder.

Peter Royal, Sok's lawyer, said the case stood alone in his thirty-six years of legal experience.

"I have never seen another case like this, and doubt we will ever see another one."

CPR 63

I n August of 1920, three Russian sheepherders thought they'd concocted the perfect plan for a train robbery. They didn't care that the high times for robbery on the Canadian Pacific Railroad through the Rocky Mountains had passed more than a decade back. The days of infamous American thief Bill Miner, the Gentleman Bandit, ended in 1911 when he fled south with the RCMP on his tail. The three Russians hadn't even immigrated to Canada until years later. Still, they'd heard stories. They received a tip that Emilio Picariello, the top bootlegger in the Crowsnest Pass, would be a passenger on the CPR 63 train. His fat wallet would make the robbery pay all on its own.

Alex Auloff, Tom Bassoff, and George Arkoff waited on the Lethbridge platform in the late afternoon of August 2. They'd bought tickets and concocted a cover story that they were labourers on their way to Fernie, British Columbia.

As the train crossed southern Alberta, the three men walked among the cars as ordinary passengers. They searched hundreds of faces to identify Picariello, better known as Emperor Pic. The Russians believed his famous face would be easy to spot.

Picariello wasn't there. The men searched again as the thick wilderness of the mountains began to pass outside the windows. No Picariello. Their plan shot, the three Russians agreed to rob the train anyway. No one on board looked as rich as Picariello, but it was worth a shot. They didn't want to lose the money they'd spent on tickets.

Ten kilometres shy of the British Columbia border, Auloff walked through the first-class car and pointed his Luger handgun in the face of conductor Sam Jones.

"This is a stick-up," Auloff said in broken, accented English.

At first, Jones thought it was a joke. The guy didn't even have a mask. He leapt for the alarm cord strung on the train car wall. Auloff fired a shot into the ceiling and Jones changed his mind. It wasn't a joke.

"Stop the train," Auloff ordered.

In the passenger cars, Bassoff and Arkoff were busy as they felt the train grind to a stop. They herded the passengers and baggage men at gunpoint toward the first-class car. The new plan was to cram as many people as possible together to keep track of them.

The gun in Bassoff's hand was heavy, a German-made Mauser with a big ammunition clip. His face was mean behind his messy hair and the thick moustache that covered his mouth. The largest of the Russians, Bassoff climbed atop the train to lock the passengers in the first-class car.

Inside the car, Auloff and Arkoff ordered the men to strip to their underwear. The pair collected wallets and watches from the men, but left the women and children alone.

Before they fled, Auloff told Jones to keep the train parked until he heard them fire a shot. Then the Russian stole the gold watch and chain from the conductor's pocket, and the thieves jumped off the train.

Disappointed, they disappeared into the thick, rocky woods near the British Columbia border. The only part of their plan to succeed was the escape. That Picariello's presence on the train was a fiction deeply hurt their take. The three Russians made off with only a few watches and $300 in bills. Auloff, at least, was pleased with the gold watch he'd taken from Jones. It would fetch him a nice profit someday.

Word of the robbery spread quickly. A nostalgic excitement took hold of people who told the story in general stores, and newspapermen breathlessly typed all the details they could scrape together.

Auloff split from Arkoff and Bassoff as a massive manhunt formed behind them. He wanted to flee south to the American border as fast as possible, but the other two wanted to stay in Alberta. Unable to compromise, Auloff went south with his share of the profits.

After a fifteen-kilometre hike in thick bush, Arkoff and Bassoff hardly kept a low profile once they reached the town of Blairmore. They spent some of their profits at a local brothel. They got drunk in the Blairmore bar and went to a town dance on Friday night. No one guessed who the two men were. There were supposed to be three of them.

The next morning, five days after the robbery of CPR 63, Arkoff and Bassoff walked the rail tracks six kilometres east to Bellevue. They were hungry, and rail towns always had a restaurant. The two strode down the main street as though they lived there. They only paused to stare at the wanted posters pasted on the office windows of the justice of the peace.

Bassoff read the description of his own messy hair, huge moustache, and height. The poster even mentioned his glass eye. Inside his office, Joseph Robertson stared out the window and recognized the men from the posters outside. Arkoff and Bassoff moved on with their stomachs still on their minds.

Robertson hurried down the street to the small RCMP detachment. Corporal Ernest Usher, a five-year policeman and Bellevue's lone Mountie, was inside. The twenty-five-year-old had immigrated to Canada and still had his Irish accent. There were two Alberta Provincial Police officers in town, the young Constable Evans Bailey and Constable James Frewin.

The three officers arrived at the Bellevue Cafe just as the Russians finished their food and started their coffee. Frewin and Usher strode through the front door and sent Bailey to cover the back. Arkoff and Bassoff sat across from each other in a booth too big for just two people. They were near the door and the pair of officers were at their table in moments.

"Hold up your hands," Usher said.

"What for?" Bassoff asked in his thick Russian accent.

"Hold them up."

Arkoff went for his gun. Frewin drew faster and fired several shots into Arkoff's right arm. Bassoff fired his large Mauser as he dove under the table. Arkoff drew his own gun with the arm he had left. Shots and smoke filled the small cafe. Twenty loud cracks.

From the front door, Usher shot Bassoff in the leg as he rolled from under the table. Bassoff fired back and hit Usher in the neck, head, and shoulder. The officer fell dead to the floor. Bailey, the youngest officer, ran inside to investigate the shots and tripped over Usher's body. Sprawled across the floor, he was shot in the head by Bassoff before he could stand again. The Russian grabbed Usher's gun as Frewin, the only officer still alive, backed out of the cafe to reload.

Arkoff was wobbling and bloody as he stood. He'd been hit with several shots after his right arm was ruined. The Russian emptied his gun into Usher's dead body. Arkoff staggered into the street and Frewin shot him again through an open window of the RCMP detachment. Arkoff went down onto the road.

Bassoff limped over to his comrade.

"I can't go any further," Arkoff said in Russian.

Bassoff shot him in the head. The remaining robber fled Frewin's final shots with a hole in his leg and a gun in each hand. He escaped Bellevue and vanished into the thick treeline at the edge of town. Frewin followed his blood trail for a quarter-mile before it disappeared.

Bassoff headed west, back toward Blairmore. He planned to hide in the remains of the Frank Slide. In 1903, a landslide had buried the mining town of Frank and killed eighty-five people. There were some rocks as big as houses to hide among in the rubble, and Bassoff thought it was his best chance on a bloody leg.

Heavy rains erased Bassoff's track and hid his smell. The big Russian had been a sheepherder for five years and knew the bush and trails well.

Behind him, the next train west carried officers from Fort Macleod and Lethbridge to join the hunt. The search party numbered almost two hundred when it was joined by local citizens. The Crowsnest Pass was filled with camps of foreign miners, and many of them traded shovels for rifles to help. The searchers brought in three bloodhounds from Seattle named Lightning, Dynamite, and Dan.

The hunters found no sign of Bassoff by the time they reached the Frank Slide. The fugitive had already stopped at the rocks to rest and bandage his leg before he entered the woods again. He broke off two branches to use as crutches.

Eventually, Bassoff reached the Holloway farmhouse near Frank. He pounded on the door and demanded food and a room. Mrs. Holloway was alone and guessed who Bassoff was at once. Scared, she gave him three pieces of bacon, as well as cheese and bread.

"Do you know who I am?" Bassoff asked her.

"No, I don't," she lied, "but I want you to leave."

Officers rushed to the Holloway farm once they heard, but Bassoff once again eluded them in the woods.

The next day, as officers and citizens searched the Crowsnest Pass, a Russian miner who had volunteered to search was mistakenly killed. Nick Kyslick was searching a vacant shack when he heard a train approach on the CPR line. He'd rushed outside and was shot dead when he failed to stop for an officer who thought he was Bassoff. Kyslick either hadn't heard or hadn't understood the commands shouted at him.

On the night of August 11, four days after the Bellevue Cafe shootout, engineer Harry Hammond manned a CPR engine as it passed through Pincher Station. There was a dishevelled man on the platform illuminated by the head-lamp as Hammond passed. Even in the middle of the night, this was nothing new. Transients often spent nights on the platforms. Usually, they waved at the train crews as they passed, but this hobo turned his face in an attempt to hide. Hammond was suspicious and thought of the hunt for Bassoff. At the next station, Hammond told the platform agent what he'd seen, and he returned to Pincher Station the same night with four police officers.

They found Bassoff on the ground behind the platform. This time he did not run. He barely moved as the officers took hold of him. They found a loaded gun in one pocket and his glass eye wrapped in paper in another. Bassoff had been on the run nine days.

In Lethbridge, the famous prisoner bragged to reporters about how close the law came in their search.

"The police were so close I could have spit on them," he said.

Bassoff was hanged in Lethbridge exactly two months later. In Ottawa, a reprieve wasn't even considered. No one believed Bassoff's story that Arkoff killed Bailey after he fell. No one believed Usher fired unprovoked to start the shootout. The hangman was called soon after the conviction.

"Goodbye, everybody," Bassoff said just before the floor fell out beneath him.

The search for Alex Auloff lasted another four years. He'd successfully made it across the American border and lived under an assumed name. Attempts to find the third Russian stalled until a gold watch and chain were pawned for $12.25 in Portland, Oregon. Investigators traced the watch stolen from conductor Sam Jones back to a gambler named Ali Hassin. The card player claimed he'd won the watch at a poker game in the town of Butte, Montana.

That's where officers found Auloff. He served seven years of his prison sentence before he died on the floor of his cell in the Prince Albert Penitentiary in Saskatchewan.

PUNKY

I t fell to Staff Sergeant Ulysses Currie of the Edmonton Police Service to deliver the awful news that ended two days of searching and started eleven years of waiting. The officer stood on a chair in the Beverly Heights police station on September 8, 1992, and took a deep breath. Roughly fifty volunteers looked up at him, though an entire city outside waited for word. More than a hundred volunteers had scoured the city for two days. They walked down alleys, combed through parks, and studied the wooded ravines bracketing the North Saskatchewan River's crooked path through the city. Some of them even waded through the sewers. Few slept. Many were parents.

"I regret to inform you we have found the body of the girl," Currie told the crowd gathered around him. "There's nothing more you can do right now, I'm afraid."

Some of the searchers burst into tears. Others cursed loudly. Most left in stunned silence.

Earlier that afternoon, Larry Rathburn returned to his trucking yard after taking the Labour Day long weekend off work. The yard was at the eastern brim of Edmonton, near the oil and gas plants on Refinery Row. Out of habit, Rathburn walked around his rig to check it for anything out of the ordinary before he got inside. When he spotted something purple on the ground beside his truck, he thought someone had left a doll in the mud. He stepped closer and saw a purple jacket.

Rathburn stopped there. The missing girl's description, including the purple jacket, was all over the news. She was face down. Rathburn went into his office and called the police. Within minutes, several cruisers sped to the trucking yard. Frigid rain began to fall over the city as officers strung yellow tape around the scene.

Soon, two helicopters hovered overhead. One carried RCMP officers, the other local reporters. Photographers perched on every nearby building to get a picture for the next day's front page. Across the yard, forensic officers pulled tarps over everything they could in an attempt to preserve evidence. There could be tire tracks, footprints, or traces of the killer on the girl's body.

Word of the grisly find spread in all directions. The search for six-year-old Corinne Gustavson was over, but the hunt for her killer had only just begun.

* * *

Two days earlier, on Sunday morning, the second-grade student at Eastwood Elementary School was playing with neighbourhood children in the yard of her family's east-end condominium. A light snow fell that morning, and her purple jacket was zipped tightly to ward off the cold. She was only steps away from her front door. Without a word, a man walked up the lane adjacent to the yard. He grabbed Corinne, hugged her, and walked away with the girl in his arms.

One of Corinne's playmates ran home to her mother, Katherine Descheneaux, in tears.

"A murderer came and got Corinne," the girl wailed.

Katherine hurried next door and knocked furiously. Corinne's father, Ray, dashed outside in his socks and ran around the parking lot. The terrified father strained to catch a glimpse of his youngest child's purple coat or her white pants with black polka dots, but couldn't find her anywhere.

The girl's kindergarten graduation photo was everywhere the next day. She wore a square burgundy cap, and her blonde hair flowed out the back to her shoulders. Her radiant smile was all teeth.

Corrine was born with wild hair that stuck straight up. One day, her grandmother looked at the infant's ridiculous hair, declaring her granddaughter looked like "one of those punkers."

From that day forward, Corinne was known to family and friends as Punky. After her death, all of Edmonton called her that as well.

* * *

The morning after Punky's body was found face down in the mud, parents across the city walked their children to school. In the Beverly area, where the Gustavsons lived, parents wouldn't even let their children play in the yard without an adult. Parents organized rotating watches at playgrounds. Many children were too scared to go outside at all.

The lone witness to the abduction, Punky's playmate, described the killer as a dark-skinned man with dark hair, three earrings, and a thin moustache. He might be driving a blue van. The description was vague, and police weren't even sure this was the right guy. Only Punky's scared young friend saw him. Officers had no idea if their suspect was a local or not. Had he just been passing by? Did he target Punky specifically?

Dozens of police officers swept entire neighbourhoods and knocked on doors, looking for anyone who seemed nervous or uncooperative. More than a hundred tips a day overloaded police phone lines during the first stage of the investigation. Thousands of dollars were donated to a reward fund. Officers stopped one man twenty-seven times in just a few days on account of his dark blue van, which was similar to the suspect vehicle.

Eight days after Punky's body was found, four hundred people packed the Evergreen Funeral Home to attend her memorial service. Her casket arrived in a horse-drawn carriage donated by a local business. Police photographers stood among the crowd, taking pictures of mourners in case the killer showed up.

"Punky has been taken from us forever by a terrible crime," Pastor Paul Knudsen said during the service. "To take someone's life this way is the most evil act that a human being could ever commit."

After the burial, Punky's aunt announced the family was starting a petition to bring back the death penalty for child killers. One Saturday later in September, Edmontonians all over the city blasted their car horns at exactly noon in organized support of Canada reinstating capital punishment. The Gustavsons' petition quickly swelled with thousands of signatures. All the Edmontonians who signed felt like they knew Punky, a girl they'd only seen on the news.

* * *

Between the pair of them, detectives Terry Alm and Al Sauve had twenty-nine years' experience as cops. Both, however, were new to the homicide unit. Punky went missing on a day when the more experienced detectives were busy with full caseloads. For the first two days, while the city hoped Punky would turn up alive, the rookie homicide detectives had little to do. They were there just in case.

Alm was at home in his kitchen making supper when the call finally came. It was Sauve.

"They found her body," he said. "I'll see you out there."

The case was massive, with fifty investigators working under Alm and Sauve. Still, the tips came in faster than officers could investigate them. Callers waited on hold for hours just to tell police about their theories. People wanted to get the guy. They wanted revenge, and the detectives were under immense pressure to make an arrest.

Weeks passed and, although detectives questioned hundreds of people, they still didn't have a clear suspect. In a bid to organize the case, police sent out fifty thousand questionnaires across northeast Edmonton in search of any viable lead. Boxes of paperwork on the Gustavson file were stacked in towers at police headquarters. Every day, officers who crossed paths with Alm and Sauve stopped them to pass on information. It was overwhelming. Cops whispered amongst themselves as the city's most infamous case remained unsolved. The two detectives often wondered if they were on the right track.

Then, they caught a lucky break. One of their suspects confessed. A mentally handicapped neighbour who used to babysit Punky. He was different than the crackpots on the tip line. He knew her.

"I'm sorry. I didn't mean to do it," he said in the interview room.

Detectives quickly realized their suspect was delusional. The details of his confession fell apart under scrutiny, and he was later admitted to a psychiatric hospital. In the observation room next door, a crowd of officers crammed inside ended their talk of champagne. A few of them cried.

Lab tests from evidence at the trucking yard, including a dark hair stuck in the mud on Punky's ankle, came up empty. Forensic officers said there wasn't enough genetic material for proper DNA tests, not with the equipment available at the time. They collected hair samples from everyone they interviewed in the hopes forensic technology would eventually catch up to their evidence, but that wouldn't pay off for years.

Alm left Alberta several times to follow up on dead-end leads in Saskatchewan, Quebec, and New Brunswick. The picture of Punky in her graduation cap went national, which led to an increase in tips, but also brought armchair detectives out of the woodwork, people convinced they'd solved the crime themselves from their couch or local coffee shop.

Some officers believed the simplest explanation, that the girl was killed by someone she knew. Her uncle, Ron Davies, was a trucker. Officers thought he seemed nervous once her body was found. It was another Hail Mary. Davies submitted to interrogation, gave DNA samples, and passed a polygraph with no trouble. Still, his innocence didn't stop strangers from making death threats against him.

The winter of 1992 melted into the spring of 1993. Alm and Sauve hadn't slept or eaten properly since the case started. The longer it went unsolved the more people pointed out that Alm and Sauve were homicide rookies.

"After a while I think you just become numb," Sauve said.

By 1994, Alm was mostly working the case solo. The fifty officers he'd started with moved on to other duties. He and Sauve picked up other homicide investigations. Punky became one victim among many.

Still, Alm kept her smiling picture tacked to the wall next to his desk.

* * *

As the years passed, Alm became convinced DNA evidence was the key. By 1996, forensics had advanced enough to re-test the pubic hair found caked in mud on the girl's ankle. The new tests produced more accurate results than in 1992, but only confirmed there was no DNA to be salvaged from the strand. After three dark and lonely years on the Punky case, Alm's hope was mostly gone.

An obsessive investigator, he was familiar with the wrongful conviction of Saskatchewan's David Milgaard, who spent two decades in prison for a rape and murder he didn't commit. Investigators finally proved his innocence when they ran DNA tests on the victim's entire underwear, rather than just fragments, and identified the real killer. Alm knew only pieces of Punky's clothing were tested. It was time to try something new. In 2000, he sent all of the girl's clothes to a genetic testing lab in North Carolina. The new technology moved slowly. It would be months before he got the results.

In March 2001, Alm's phone rang.

"Has your victim got any boyfriends?" the voice from North Carolina asked. The lab wanted to make sure what they'd found wasn't innocent.

"Well, she was a six-year-old girl," Alm replied.

"I've got your killer."

The tests produced a DNA profile, though not a name. Still, it was invaluable. Alm compared the killer's DNA with samples gathered from suspects over the years. None of them matched, but on the other hand, nearly four hundred suspects were eliminated. For the first time in years, there was a sharp focus to the case.

At the time, Canada was taking its first steps toward a national DNA databank to catalogue criminal profiles for comparison in unsolved cases. Across the country, prosecutors were getting court orders to take samples from violent predators already in the prison system.

If Punky's killer had ever hurt anyone else, ever been caught, it was only a matter of time.

* * *

Inside his cell at the Bowden Institution in central Alberta, forty-year-old Clifford Sleigh was worried. Like many men imprisoned in the medium-security institution, Sleigh recognized what the national DNA databank meant. He could connect the dots.

Investigators had questioned Sleigh in 1993 about Punky Gustavson, and he'd cooperated. Sleigh was in Edmonton for a softball tournament on the same day she vanished, staying with family who lived near the Gustavson home, but police lost interest in Sleigh as a suspect after his common-law wife gave him an alibi. He raped a girl a year after Punky's death, then another in 1994. He was convicted and sentenced to fifteen years in prison for those crimes.

None of Sleigh's DNA remained on file from the rape investigations, but as he was a serial sexual offender, it wasn't long before officers wanted another sample from him. They took his blood in December 2002 at the Bowden Institution infirmary. Prison staff said the convicted rapist became depressed soon after.

A month later, police matched Sleigh's sample with the DNA found on Punky's purple jacket. They finally had the evidence to close the case.

The public announcement came in March 2003, more than a decade after Punky went outside to play in her front yard. Police charged Clifford Sleigh with first-degree murder, kidnapping, and aggravated sexual assault in the death of Corinne Gustavson. He was later convicted on all counts.

Alm was retired by the time police finally broke the case, but received an invitation to attend the announcement from colleagues who respected his work and tireless dedication to seeking justice for Punky. He stood alongside crying members of the Gustavson family.

"This is the best day I've had in over a decade," he said.

THE KIDNAPPING
OF HYMAN BELZBERG

Despite his millions, Hyman Belzberg still swept the floor of his family's furniture store in his shirt and tie. His black Lincoln Continental pulled into the parking lot behind the Cristy's Arcade store five or six days a week, always at 7:45 a.m. Belzberg had run the store on 11th Street in Calgary for decades, since before his family's small holdings grew to a $2.7 billion empire across North America. The store was his second home as a child. His father, Abraham, opened the doors after he immigrated from Poland, where he had worked as a fishmonger, in 1919. The store remained the cornerstone of the Belzberg finances for years, and in 1945 Abraham handed the keys to the oldest of his three sons.

"You're on your own, mister," he told Hyman.

Belzberg lived his entire life in Calgary. He and his children attended Flames games at the Stampede Corral arena, and Belzberg took long walks with his wife in Glenmore Park. With his money, he could've built a home anywhere in the world, perhaps in a larger, warmer city like his brothers did. Instead, he stayed home.

For Belzberg, a tall man with a ring of white hair, the only drawback to his dedication was that anyone could know where he'd be at a certain time each day.

On Thursday, December 9, 1982, Belzberg pulled into the Cristy's Arcade lot in the dim light of dawn and parked near a grey 1977 Chevrolet van with orange stripes. Two armed men in masks jumped him as he stepped from the car. The multi-millionaire recognized the abduction attempt and fought back. As the three men struggled, Cristy's Arcade employees and people waiting for the bus stared in shock at what they thought was a mugging.

Belzberg fought with the strength of a younger man until they slammed him into the van's frame hard enough to break a rib.

Carl Woodcock, one of the furniture store's drivers, ran across the parking lot toward his boss.

"Help me, Woody, help me," Belzberg yelled from inside the van.

One of the masked men turned and raised his gun. "Get back!"

Woodcock skidded to a stop and watched helplessly as the van's doors slammed shut and a third man behind the wheel squealed out of the parking lot.

"I'm going to take this gun if you resist and blow your leg off," one of the kidnappers told Belzberg as the van bounced over a curb.

Woodcock leapt into one of the Cristy's Arcade trucks, but lost the van in the rush hour traffic clogging 11th Street. Belzberg was gone.

Witnesses were of little help to investigators. Some said the van was grey, and others swore it was black. Perhaps there were rainbow stripes on the side. Officers pulled over every van they found on 11th Street, but none of them had a millionaire in the back.

Only Woodcock gave the police an accurate description. That night, his wife shook him awake because he was describing the van in his sleep.

Detectives knew immediately what had happened. A man of Belzberg's wealth was taken for only one reason. Though he was among the richest men in Calgary, police knew they couldn't count on Belzberg to be recognized by strangers. He was too rich to be anonymous, but too quiet to be famous. Hyman was not the high roller his younger brothers were: Bill, in Los Angeles, and Samuel, in Vancouver, who ran the family's real estate and banking empire.

In his personal life, Belzberg owned the Lincoln and a forty-two-acre estate in Calgary. During business hours, he worked hard for every dollar, same as his father. Abraham Belzberg's first son knew no one succeeded in business by giving something away. Some people called Hyman cheap. He once invited a Toronto furniture dealer for lunch and gave him half a cheese sandwich pulled from his desk.

Friends told investigators Belzberg wasn't afraid of anything. He'd served in the Canadian Navy during the Second World War. Once, on his own, he'd chased down a small group of thieves that broke into the furniture store.

The Belzberg family gathered at Hyman's southwest Calgary estate as they waited for the inevitable ransom call. Samuel, the top man in the family's businesses, flew in from Vancouver on his private jet. Bill, the youngest, boarded the first flight out of Los Angeles. Hyman's three adult children and his wife, Jennie, opened their home to police officers who stood beside their phones. Other officers were posted at Cristy's Arcade.

Police quickly quelled rumours that the kidnapping was political. The Belzbergs were known to give generously to Jewish causes, including the Simon Wiesenthal Center for Holocaust Studies. The centre was renowned for hunting Nazi war criminals across the world. The family had lost many relatives in Second World War concentration camps after Abraham moved to Canada. This kidnapping was too sloppy for international heavyweights.

The first break in the case came four hours after the abduction. The grey van with orange stripes was found abandoned in an alley behind Miller's Stereo, four blocks from the furniture store. The van had been stolen from a dealership on Macleod Trail the night before. Police figured the kidnappers must have swapped vehicles soon after the kidnapping. No way they would risk being on foot.

As police chased down leads from the stolen van, Belzberg was handcuffed, chained, and blindfolded in a southwest Calgary home. A mass of wires and some type of clay were strapped to his chest. Michael Nobleman, the lead kidnapper, told Belzberg it was a bomb.

Nobleman thought his plan had gone well despite a few glitches. They'd slept in and nearly missed Belzberg in the parking lot. Gregory Hedch, brought in as a driver at the last minute, briefly got lost after the grab. Still, they hadn't been forced to fire their guns, and now their target was on the floor in Nobleman's house, two kilometres from Belzberg's own estate.

The young Hedch was only recruited because he was the brother-in-law of Nobleman's partner in planning, Avrom Raber. Hedch would do anything Raber said.

A few months earlier, the twenty-three-year-old Nobleman had lost $180,000 in investments. Raber, his older cousin, feared he'd become suicidal in the wake of his losses. When Nobleman created the plot to seize Belzberg, Raber agreed to help. They planned hastily and drove by Cristy's Arcade only twice before the kidnapping. They collected two handguns, an automatic rifle, and a few fake guns and hand grenades. Six hundred bullets were piled around Nobleman's home, all paid for by the proceeds of a Safeway grocery store robbery the week before.

In the afternoon, Nobleman left to call Belzberg's lawyer from a phone booth. It was the first of several calls from pay phones Nobleman would make through the afternoon and evening. Mostly, he spoke to Samuel as the worried brother paced Hyman's home. Nobleman demanded $7 million in American, Swiss, and West German currencies. Samuel said he could only get $2 million on short notice. Hyman's brother did his best to extend the calls long enough for police to trace them. No one in the Belzberg home slept well.

Across the Atlantic Ocean, neither did George Adolph Faust. The fourth man in the kidnapping plot had been in Switzerland for days. Nobleman recruited the fifty-eight-year-old businessman after they met at a Calgary car dealership because Faust spoke German and had experience with Swiss banking. He'd been a German pilot in the Second World War until he was captured by the Russians. Along with Nobleman, Faust had made poor choices in the stock market in the last few weeks.

With $17,000 from the Safeway robbery, Faust opened an account in the town of Frauenfeld to hold the anticipated ransom money. The plan was for him to withdraw the cash in Swiss francs and deposit them into another account in Liechtenstein. Nobleman updated Faust between his negotiation calls with the Belzbergs.

In the middle of the afternoon, at dawn in Calgary, Faust called Nobleman and reported that $1.8 million in Canadian funds had been transferred to Switzerland, but hadn't yet reached Frauenfeld. Employees at the small-town bank doubted they could produce four million francs on a Friday afternoon.

Nobleman asked if he should release Belzberg.

No, Faust told him. The money could be frozen unless the cash was moved first.

Faust said they should wait, but Nobleman didn't. Nearly twenty-four hours after grabbing Belzberg, his captors dropped him off in a shopping mall parking lot near Nobleman's home.

Belzberg called his family from the nearest phone and told them the ordeal was over. Immediately, Samuel called his banker to freeze the ransom money before Faust could withdraw any of it.

Once home, Belzberg called the manager of Cristy's Arcade, David Ritchie.

"He said he thought he might take the day off," Ritchie recalled. "I told him I hoped he'd take a few days."

Later that morning, police traced a suspect phone call to Nobleman's home. He, Hedch, and Raber surrendered after a brief, quiet standoff in the southwest neighbourhood. In the afternoon, the three of them appeared in an Calgary courtroom's prisoner's box in their street clothes.

As reporters and lawyers stared at the three failed kidnappers, Hyman Belzberg boarded his brother's private jet to seclude himself in Samuel's Vancouver mansion. A fleet of Cadillacs picked up the family at the Vancouver airport and drove behind the high iron gates of one of the city's largest homes.

As he stepped from one of the cars, Hyman waved at the reporters gathered at the gates.

"Thank you," he called out. "I'm fine."

On Monday morning, at 7:45, Hyman Belzberg pulled his Lincoln into his Calgary furniture store's parking lot and returned to work.

"Things are back to normal, hopefully, today," he said. "I'm fine and it's business as usual. I'm glad to be out."

His twenty-four hours of captivity were only violent in the first minutes. They struck me, he said, and I struck back. They weren't going to take me easily, he told the *Calgary Herald*.

As Belzberg worked, Faust gave himself up in Switzerland once he heard authorities were searching for him.

A week later, Faust waived his extradition hearing and was escorted back to Canada by a Calgary detective. On the long flight, he turned to the officer with tears in his eyes.

"I should have known," Faust said. "I knew that day we'd be caught."

Nobleman, Hedch, and Raber pleaded guilty to kidnapping, conspiracy, and extortion. Faust was convicted after a short trial.

Their own lawyers portrayed them as "buffoons" who had created an ill-conceived, sloppy plan. They weren't criminals, court heard, just desperate men.

"It was a bizarre and unbelievable type of scheme that was doomed to failure," said Larry Ross, Nobleman's lawyer.

Raber's lawyer argued the forethought of the ridiculous plan did not mean his client was in his right mind.

"Even the Marx brothers' films required planning and timing," he said.

"I WILL FIND YOU"

On July 13, 2005, Michael James White stared into a news camera from the living room couch at his north Edmonton home and did his best to break the city's heart. With a cracked voice and teary eyes, he tried to speak to his wife more than twenty-four hours after she disappeared. His pudgy face was contorted with grief.

"Liana," he wailed. "Hold tight. If whoever has her, or if she is out there and you see me, just stay there and we will find you. I will find you.

"She would never hurt a fly," he added. "She is a gentle person."

Later, accompanied by detectives, the former soldier walked outside to meet the media horde in his driveway clad in sandals, shorts, and a T-shirt. Michael's shaved head towered a least a foot taller than those of the investigators who came out of his light grey home.

"Thanks to everybody who's been involved and looking. Thank you. Thanks for every police officer and detective on the case. Thank you. I just want to say thanks."

The twenty-nine-year-old turned and scuffled along the manicured lawn and through the yellow flowers near the front door back inside the house. A detective put a supportive hand on his shoulder.

Reporters called their newsrooms on cellphones that appeared the moment Michael was gone. At the time, his family was the biggest story in the city. A photo of Liana, with her beaming smile and long, brown hair was everywhere. Everyone had a theory about what had happened to her.

The previous morning, shortly before 6:00 a.m., Liana White's Ford Explorer was found in the otherwise empty parking lot of a baseball diamond a kilometre and a half from their home. The driver's door was wide open, and her purse and keys were still inside. Her wallet was missing, though her driver's licence and other cards were strewn on the ground. Outside the vehicle, Liana's cellphone was found next to her shoes, placed neatly side by side. There were no drag marks, no signs of struggle. There was no blood and no Liana dressed in her hospital scrubs. She hadn't arrived that morning at the Royal Alexandra Hospital, where she worked in the neonatal intensive care unit.

The Whites met in 1998, seven years before, at an Edmonton nightclub. At the time, Michael was a Canadian Forces trooper stationed at the Edmonton Garrison and Liana was a recent arrival from Kelowna, British Columbia. They married less than two years later. At first the couple lived in military housing, and later with Liana's mother before their bank account grew enough for them to buy their own home. Their daughter, Ashley, was now two years old. Liana was pregnant with their second child the day she disappeared.

The marriage had some problems, as all marriages do. Finances were tight, but not impossible. Michael's screwups over the years caused some turmoil in their home. He'd twice been caught stealing from the army and spent weeks confined to barracks. Michael eventually quit the army and started a new career as a heavy-duty mechanic. As far as anyone around them knew, the family was now contented as they awaited their second child.

Liana left for work early Wednesday morning before he woke up, Michael said. He'd later gone to work, but police called him home after Liana's vehicle was found. As officers watched, Michael cried and filled out a missing person report at his kitchen table.

She's four months pregnant, he told them. The baby was due at Christmas.

The house was in pristine shape. All the tables and countertops were clear, and the floor was spotless.

One of the detectives asked Michael if he was hiding anything from them.

"How could you ask me that?" Michael said. "I loved her. I still love her. I'm talking in the past tense now. All day I've been thinking that."

He told police he didn't want to speak to reporters about the search for his wife.

"You know, it's a private matter," he said a day before his tearful pleas were on television.

That first night, Liana's mother, Maureen Kelly, paced the home in a panic as she thought of where her daughter could be, if someone had taken her. Michael sat on the couch, turned on the television, and fell asleep. He snored loudly.

In the morning, Michael told investigators he hadn't slept for even a minute.

The entire situation made little sense to Detective Michael Campeau.

Liana, an only child, lived a careful life. She always locked doors behind her as she went through her daily routine. Friends said Liana would grasp their hands when a stranger approached. Women like that weren't easily taken.

The pair of Liana's shoes outside her Ford bothered Campeau. They were dropped so precisely beside each other. Not kicked up or dragged off. The driver's seat of the Explorer was adjusted far back from the steering wheel. An officer almost six feet tall could barely touch the gas pedal, and Liana was six inches shorter.

To Campeau, the scene at the baseball diamond parking lot looked staged.

On Thursday, the official line was that Liana's case was still only a missing person file.

"We have no indication at all that a crime has taken place, if in fact she has been abducted, assaulted or anything at all," Inspector Jamie Ewatski told reporters. "We don't have that."

Soon, they did. Investigators put Michael under surveillance. Their suspicion of the grieving husband turned to certainty when officers scanning local surveillance camera tapes watched one from the nearby Richard's Pub. The tape showed Liana's Explorer headed away from the house on Wednesday morning, toward the ball diamond shortly before it was discovered empty. More than ten minutes later, a man who looked a lot like Michael ran past the camera in the other direction. The video was too fuzzy to be conclusive, but detectives were sure.

Investigators didn't rush in. There was still no indication of where Liana might be. They needed to let Michael believe he was getting away with it, let him make his own choices that might lead to more clues. They didn't tell him about the video. They stood by and watched him give more media interviews.

"My sorrow has now become anger," Michael told another television camera. He said he wanted to start a search of his own.

Investigators said he could, though an officer managed the volunteer efforts.

Officers covertly followed Michael to a deserted field near his house that evening. He crept around a chain-link fence, walked through waist-high grass, emerged with a full garbage bag in each hand, and put them in his truck. Later, Michael tossed the bags on the curb for garbage pickup. A police officer grabbed them out of the garbage truck the next morning.

The bags were full of evidence. There was a broken lampshade that matched the one in the Whites' bedroom. Officers found Liana's bloody pants, as well as sponges, latex gloves covered with more blood, and one of Michael's T-shirts stained with even more. Again, police didn't let Michael know what they'd found.

That day, Michael led his own search of volunteers, friends, and family members. Police and search dogs joined them, and helicopters hovered overhead. He kept in close touch with detectives and asked their advice on how to find Liana three days after she'd last been seen. Inside the White home, officers combed through each room after Michael gave them permission.

The next evening, it was Michael himself who found Liana's body. He led a team of searchers who discovered her remains in a ditch northeast of the city, partially buried by branches and brown leaves beside a gravel road. Michael quickly spotted the dolphin tattoo on her left ankle. There were stab wounds on her body.

Michael dropped to his knees in the marshy ditch and wept. Someone called police.

When homicide investigators arrived, Michael told them to photograph the licence plates of passing cars because killers often returned to the scene of their crimes.

"Arrest him," Campeau told his officers shortly after Liana was found. "Arrest him for murder."

I knew it, said people across Edmonton.

Michael denied everything in a downtown interview room with Detective Ernie Schreiber. He ate a ham-and-cheese sandwich and insisted that his daughter broke the lampshade found in the garbage bags and the bloody items were from a nosebleed.

Schreiber showed him the video from Richard's Pub.

"That's you, Mike," the officer said. "Want to see it again?"

"That's not me," Michael protested. "That's my Explorer. That's not me running. There's just no possible way."

Michael sat silently for a long time and then became angry and accusatory as the interview ended. "Is this because I found her and you guys couldn't? Is it because I went searching?"

Michael never admitted to anything. He'd only picked up the garbage bags from a random field as a good citizen, he said. Littering was a crime he'd rectified.

"I wish you'd believe me."

No one did. When Michael was released on bail months later, six hundred people in his neighbourhood signed a petition to have him sent back to jail to await trial. No one wanted to be anywhere near him. His daughter, Ashley, lived with Liana's mother.

Fourteen months later, it took a jury ten hours to declare Michael White guilty.

HIRED MAN

Jasper Collins met the weeping widow as she stepped off a passenger train and onto the wooden platform in Kindersley, Saskatchewan.

A month had passed since she'd last seen her husband, an American lawyer named John Benson. He and Collins, a young hired man, left Missouri in April 1913 and headed north to stake a land claim in the new province of Alberta. Benson planned to build a home, and his wife was to follow four weeks later. He'd sent letters to the United States nearly every day to his wife about their land outside the small town of Cereal in southeast Alberta. Mrs. Benson left Missouri on May 3 to meet her husband in Saskatoon before they travelled across the provincial border to their newly constructed home. Their young son would eventually join them after staying with relatives in Missouri.

John Benson wasn't there when his wife stepped off the train in Saskatoon. For days, she waited alone and worried in a single room at the King Edward Hotel on Avenue A. On May 7, a telegram arrived that said her husband had burned to death in their new home. The telegram told her to meet Collins at Kindersley.

The skinny eighteen-year-old waited there with her husband's burned corpse inside a metal coffin packed in a shipping crate.

"Oh Jasper, what has happened?"

Collins told her the story he'd practiced. That day, he'd been in the pasture pouring water for Benson's new horses when he heard an explosion. The shack he and Benson lived in while they built the home was nearly two kilometres away and was aflame by the time he returned, Collins said. There hadn't been anyone else around. He ran to the nearest neighbours for help, but the shack was a smouldering wreck before anything could be done. The oil lamp must have exploded, Collins said. There was no other explanation. Her husband of eight years was in bed and died there, he told Benson's widow.

Royal Northwest Mounted Police investigators in Alberta declared the blaze accidental. The investigation had ended after Benson's body was found near the charred oil lamp.

Collins swore none of Benson's money was found in the burnt wood and ash that remained. Benson had slept with his pocketbook of twenty-dollar bills under his pillow and his coat over his head. His savings burned with him, the hired man said.

Collins paid for his train ticket to Kindersley with twenty-two dollars a cousin loaned him, he said.

Mrs. Benson believed every word, and the pair headed south to Missouri with her husband in a box.

* * *

In the small Missouri town of Braymer, Collins was as reviled as Benson had been popular. Collins came from a poor family that lived in a dilapidated house on the outskirts of town. His father had died years before, and Jasper was the oldest of three siblings. Before the trip to Canada, Collins was charged with what newspapers called an "unmentionable crime" against his sister. Benson represented him in court and Collins was acquitted. Later, Benson hired Collins to help him move to Canada. No one else in Braymer would give Collins a job. The acquittal hadn't silenced the rumours.

For three months, people wondered. Benson's fellow Freemasons were suspicious about his death. Constable

James Burnette of Caldwell County kept his eye on Collins. The skinny kid appeared to have a lot more money to spend since he'd returned from Alberta. The Freemasons exhumed Benson's body for examination when Collins refused to answer further questions about his boss's death.

A doctor studied the corpse and found a hole between the fourth and fifth ribs. There was trauma to the remains of the heart that fire couldn't explain. Also, the skull was damaged and missing a tooth on the left side. It appeared he'd been hit in the head and shot in the heart, the doctor concluded.

The next morning, on August 10, Burnette called at the house where Collins lived with his mother.

"Jasper, I want to see you for a moment."

Burnette arrested him at the front door as his mother watched. The officer searched the bedroom Collins had slept in his whole life. There was $1,800 in twenties inside a trunk in the corner.

Burnette held up the money.

It was from land he'd sold in Canada, Collins explained.

Burnette asked more questions about the land Collins supposedly once owned. Who bought the land? What was the precise cost of the sale? Why were all the profits from a Canadian sale in American currency?

Collins had no answers. He admitted it was Benson's money after less than an hour of questions.

Collins offered the constable a deal on the way to the county jail in Kingston, Missouri. If the constable would allow him one last night at his family home, he would say how Benson really died.

Burnette agreed and turned his prisoner around. In his house, Collins recited his confession in front of Burnette and a Pinkerton detective. Collins scrawled his name across the bottom.

Collins wrote that he and Benson were nearly finished a rough house on the land near Cereal when he attacked Benson with a blow to the head. Collins then grabbed the lawyer's own .38-calibre pistol and shot him in the chest as he lay on the floor of their sleeping shack. Collins stole Benson's money from under his pillow, splashed lamp oil across the wooden walls, and set the fire to disguise his crime.

Benson actually did owe him $200 of the stolen money, Collins added.

"You know the trouble I was in with my sister?" Collins asked Burnette. "I am not guilty of that, but I am guilty of the murder of Benson."

In Braymer, word spread quickly among people who already suspected Collins of killing Benson. Benson was well-liked, and there was talk of hanging Collins that day. Burnette told the townspeople Collins would face justice in Canada, where he committed the crime. Still, the lawman watched his prisoner carefully until he was taken north.

Authorities transported Collins nearly twenty-five hundred kilometres to face a murder charge at the Royal Northwest Mounted Police barracks in Calgary.

It was a simple trial once Justice Horace Harvey decided Collins' confession was voluntary. The confession was read aloud to the jury as Collins sat quiet and slack in the packed courtroom.

The jury convicted the hired hand, and Harvey sentenced him to death.

"I feel no doubt, in my own mind, that the verdict is absolutely correct," the judge told the court. "The only way in which crime can be prevented is by the proper punishment of those who commit the crime. There is only one sentence I can impose, and that is the sentence of death."

Collins was set to hang on February 17, 1914. During the month before his execution, his life was miserable. He barely spoke for the entire four weeks. He was straitjacketed and tied to his bed after he tossed a full waste pail down death row. He chewed his blankets and attempted to bite people who came within his reach. He refused to eat, and guards forced milk and gruel down his throat, according to the prison journal of his stay.

On the day of his execution at the Calgary barracks, Collins woke early and wrote a letter to his mother in Missouri.

Collins was executed in private, away from public eyes, but the details of his botched death were revealed in a coroner's report later that day.

The executioner mistakenly cut Collins down while he was still alive. His neck was gruesomely dislocated as he struggled for breath in front of official witnesses. The young man's misery lasted so long prison officials discussed hanging him a second time.

Twelve minutes later, Collins died with a doctor's finger on the pulse of his neck.

DAR

Darlene Heatherington was missing.

The Lethbridge alderman vanished on May 3, 2003, from Great Falls, Montana, while on a business trip. Heatherington and others on Lethbridge city council were south of the border for several days of municipal meetings. While her fellow aldermen returned home to southern Alberta on Friday, Heatherington decided to stay for an extra day of American shopping. She called her husband, David, at home with their three young children, and promised she'd return safely to Lethbridge later that night. She lamented missing their children's piano recital. David offered to videotape it for her.

David called police when his wife didn't arrive in Lethbridge as scheduled. Word spread quickly that the politician was missing.

"We're taking it moment by moment, one step at a time," David told a reporter on the Heatheringtons' front step.

Across the border, in Great Falls, one of the twelve detectives assigned to the case found Heatherington's rented Ford Focus parked in the town's civic centre lot. The thirty-nine-year-old's wallet, jacket, and cellphone were still inside. Her keys were on the pavement beneath the vehicle. The Montana officers discovered she'd spent ten dollars on a used mountain bike at a pawn shop, and the small woman was last seen pedalling toward the paths along the river. Officers searched desperately along the banks of the

Missouri River for any sign of the woman known to family and friends as Dar.

"We're putting a lot of effort into this," said Lieutenant Steffens of the Great Falls Police Department. "It's priority number one."

At the Heatherington home, the phone rang constantly with messages of support.

People began to assume the worst had happened.

It was all bullshit.

Three days after she vanished, Heatherington was found outside the Treasure Island Hotel on the Las Vegas strip. Blurry and disoriented, she told police officers in the Nevada city she'd been drugged, sexually assaulted, and abducted from Great Falls. Given the ordeal she'd been through, investigators were surprised when she became uncooperative and argumentative. Half her answers were evasive, and the rest were contradictory.

Officers brought her to a Las Vegas hospital, but Heatherington stopped a medical examination before doctors could determine if she was injured. The alderman said she couldn't remember a thing about her abductor. Exasperated, she told Las Vegas investigators she would answer their questions after she slept. Instead, she rushed to the airport with David after he'd chartered a flight from Alberta. Heatherington flew back to Montana without speaking to officers again.

Detectives in Great Falls were eager to hear about the attacker who'd preyed in their town. Through tears, Heatherington told them a stranger approached her from behind in the civic centre parking lot, snaked his arm around her neck, and stabbed a syringe into her arm. She woke up handcuffed in a car on the way to Nevada, she said.

Officers untangled enough lies in their first forty-five minutes with her to accuse Heatherington of making it all up. She then changed her story, claiming she'd met a married man from Alberta on a Missouri River trail and they'd run away to Las Vegas together.

Great Falls authorities charged her with providing false information to police. Two weeks later, she was fined one hundred dollars for court costs and ordered to seek psychiatric help. It seemed to put an end to the lies. Heatherington went home and waited for the newspaper headlines to fade. The reprieve was short-lived. In June, Lethbridge police charged her with public mischief.

Months before her trip to Great Falls, Heatherington filed a police report claiming she had a stalker who harassed her with obscene phone calls. In the course of investigating her complaint, police tapped the phones at her home and office to try and catch the stalker in the act. Almost immediately, the phone calls stopped, and sexually explicit letters began to arrive.

Heatherington claimed the pornographic notes were left in her home mailbox, at her office, and under the windshield wipers of her vehicle. Each one happened to arrive when police weren't watching.

Surveillance cameras at Dar's home recorded no suspicious stalkers. Police noticed the notes that kept arriving contained personal details only those closest to Heatherington would know. When surveillance tapes contradicted her story about finding a note in her home, the alderman suddenly remembered she'd actually found it on her windshield. Police caught her looking at library books on stalking that contained phrases repeated in the notes.

As police investigated, Heatherington took self-defence classes. Against all police advice, Heatherington still went for long runs alone near the Oldman River.

Lethbridge officers first accused her of creating her own stalker the day before she left for Great Falls. Officers told her the investigation into her fictions took eight months and cost the department $17,000. Police in Great Falls concluded Heatherington planned every detail of her false abduction to convince Lethbridge police her stalker was real.

Lethbridge officers told her their investigation proved no stalker ever existed. In an interview room, Heatherington did all she could to save herself.

"While revealing nothing to the interrogator, the accused puts on a bravura performance of wronged innocence, faintly damning her husband and trying desperately to find out how much the police know," a judge later wrote.

On her fortieth birthday, Heatherington held a press conference and painted herself as the victim. She returned to her original story—she'd been drugged, assaulted, and taken to Las Vegas against her will. In this version, a man she'd met at the edge of the Missouri River offered her a bottle of water that contained the drugs. Police in Great Falls forced her to say she'd lied about her disappearance, she claimed.

"They wanted to hear me say that I had an affair," she told media in a rambling, defensive speech. "They wanted to hear me say that I had planned it."

Through the summer of 2003, Heatherington faced widespread pressure to resign from city council. One alderman pushed a motion, unsuccessfully, that council officially demand her resignation. Newspapers and coffee shop gossip speculated that the combative Heatherington spent more of her expense account than any other local politician.

Angry phone calls swamped Lethbridge City Hall. Constituents complained about her continued position and the embarrassing national attention she'd drawn to Lethbridge. However, the council was powerless to fire her even after a meeting in which she furiously accused them of cowardice for denying her a temporary turn as deputy mayor. Her fellow aldermen just wanted her to leave with what little grace remained.

In January 2004, Heatherington's public mischief trial was a circus that dominated the town of seventy-three thousand for three weeks. She made a salacious return to the front page, and every detail received national coverage. The courtroom was filled with as many fascinated onlookers as there were journalists. A minor charge in most other circumstances became a daily soap opera that hooked thousands each day.

Heatherington's defence tossed the blame onto her husband of seventeen years, a dignified, soft-spoken firefighter who stood beside his wife through the many months of controversy. Each morning, David walked the media gauntlet into the courthouse hand in hand with his wife. Once inside, her lawyers made him the accused. They suggested he'd invented his wife's stalker due to petty jealousy of her success as a municipal politician. It was he who created the letters and terrified his wife, court heard, even though he'd been in Calgary when some of the letters arrived.

Provincial court Judge Peter Caffaro saw through it all.

"I found that Mrs. Heatherington was not to be trusted to tell the truth," he told court as she cried beside her lawyer.

Heatherington herself obviously wrote the letters from her supposed stalker, Caffaro said, including those copied verbatim from books she'd read in the local library.

Less than a month later, she resigned her seat on Lethbridge city council in a move unanimously accepted by her colleagues. Weeks later, Caffaro sentenced her to eight months of house arrest. She was allowed no visitors besides her family and could leave only to attend church and shop for groceries.

As they left the Lethbridge courthouse for the last time, David still held Dar's hand.

THE DOCTORS OF FAIRVIEW

The constant tension in the Fairview Health Complex had little to do with patients and emergencies. The insults and animosity in the corridors were all among the staff at the northwestern Alberta hospital. The health complex had four doctors, and one of them was not like the others.

Dr. Abraham Robert Cooper moved to Fairview in 1989. The father of two was already an experienced doctor when he arrived. At sixty, he'd been a doctor for twenty-five years, both as a member of the Canadian Forces and as a civilian. He'd treated patients as a surgeon and general practitioner in Calgary and in small towns scattered across Montana, North Dakota, and Minnesota. Through those years, he'd also received his pilot's licence, purchased a plane, and earned black belts in jiu-jitsu and tae kwon do. Doctors who worked with Cooper praised his medical skills, but some were glad to see him go.

Cooper began to make more enemies shortly after he moved to Fairview. He thought the three current doctors–Dr. Doug Snider, Dr. Soong-Yo Chung, and Dr. John Edward Clarke–were incompetent and apathetic to patients. He loudly told them so whenever he could. Compared to him, Cooper thought, they were not doctors. Cooper's blunt, antagonistic opinions quickly turned other staff against him and dominated daily life in the hospital. The doctors filed complaints against each other and fought over patient treatment. Once, colleagues accused Cooper of throwing a pair of bloody scissors at a nurse during surgery because they were too dull.

It was no secret. Many people in Fairview, a town of thirty-eight hundred people, witnessed the arguments and told many others who hadn't.

By March 1994, the hospital board was fed up and terminated Cooper's hospital privileges. The board told the black-belt doctor the disruptions in the hospital were his fault.

"Cooper's continued presence within the Fairview Health Complex has been and would be disruptive and detrimental," the board stated. "Too much animosity has been generated having regard to Dr. Cooper's general attitude and his opinions regarding the medical staff and of the entire administration."

Cooper was furious. The board would be better off if they banned Snider, Chung, and Clarke and kept him in the hospital halls, he said. Any complaints his fellow doctors filed against him were only evidence of their lack of ethics.

For five years, Cooper fought the decision with his usual force. The board was biased against him, he repeated. The other three doctors just wanted him run out of town. In the meantime, Cooper opened his own clinic in Fairview and stayed clear of the hospital.

The same month Cooper lost the final appeal for his hospital privileges, he launched a $3.2 million civil suit against his three fellow doctors. They had plotted an illegal conspiracy to destroy him. For months, Cooper told anyone who'd listen that he'd ruin the other doctors for what they'd done.

Chung became frightened when his wife swore she saw Cooper drive slowly past their home and stare inside. Chung told police that Cooper called and offered him protection in the lawsuit if he switched sides. Chung hung up on him.

Snider was the most worried of all. He'd been a doctor in Fairview for thirty years and never met anyone like Cooper. Snider was scheduled to testify in the lawsuit in a few months. Privately, Snider told people the legal fight had become desperate. At a Conservative political convention,

Snider talked to a member of the Legislative Assembly he knew from Leduc.

"He said if things kept going the way they were, he could not see it going for more than four or five months," Albert Klapstein told reporters. "I'll kill him or he'll kill me."

On May 5, 1999, Snider watched the evening news and worked on an oil painting until his phone rang around nine o'clock. He spoke for a few minutes, hung up, and went to the bedroom to talk to his wife, Jean.

"That telephone call, that was Abe," he said.

Cooper wanted to meet that night to talk about the ongoing lawsuit. The relationship between Cooper and Snider had been the worst at the hospital. They'd fought constantly. Snider talked to Jean numerous times about his problems with Cooper. Snider came to one conclusion.

"There's got to be rules."

Snider, a father of three, left his home on foot to meet Cooper. No one ever saw him again.

Jean Snider woke in the middle of the night and realized her husband hadn't returned home. She called the RCMP at sunrise.

Around the same time, a five-hour drive south, Cooper said goodbye to his wife in the Edmonton International Airport parking lot. He was headed to an American College for Advancement in Medicine conference in Florida. Cooper handed his wife an envelope to give to the lawyer handling his lawsuit and boarded his flight. The doctor left his grey Nissan Maxima in the airport parking lot. There were red trickles over the back bumper and tail lights.

In Fairview, word and fear spread quickly. Snider was a popular neighbour and doctor in town. People lined up to say good things about him to the Edmonton reporters who crowded Fairview to cover the mystery.

More than three hundred people began to search a day after the doctor was last seen. Snider had helped some of the searchers deliver their babies. Some of the searchers were those babies, who had grown up with Snider as their doctor. They met each morning on Fairview's main street and split into teams of three to cover the many highways and secondary roads around the town. No one harboured any hope that Snider was simply lost. On his mountain bike, Snider was known to visit the patches of farmland he owned in the area. He knew the roads well.

"I would like nothing better than if he walked through the door and said he had bumped his head," said Darren Snider, Doug's thirty-six-year-old son, "but I don't think it looks very good."

Snider's disappearance put the town on edge even before police declared any foul play. Many needed no reminder of the conflict among the town's doctors. Suspicion fell upon Cooper, while other residents defended him and condemned the whispers.

And where was Cooper anyway? Though RCMP investigators knew he went to Florida, others in Fairview had no idea. It now appeared to be a double missing-persons case and an even greater mystery to Fairview's residents.

Cooper returned from Florida five days after Snider vanished. Investigators later said the doctor must have known he was a suspect when he returned to Canada as if nothing was wrong. RCMP officers met him at the airport with search warrants for his clothes, luggage, and car. Officers quickly spotted bloodstains on Cooper's shirt, pants, and shoes. In the parking lot, police found the red streaks on the bumper of the Nissan. The trunk was damp with blood. Police seized Cooper's car and clothes.

Still, no body. No arrest. Cooper returned to Fairview on his own.

Volunteer searchers around Fairview began to go home for good the same day Cooper returned to Alberta. Five days had gone by with no sign. Snider's friends and family, as well as RCMP officers and their German shepherds, kept on. It was widely agreed they were now looking for a body.

On May 10, even dedicated searchers paused to hold a memorial for Snider. Ten days was too long for hope. Eight hundred people crammed themselves into a Fairview church for their farewells.

Hazel Magnussen addressed the crowd, but spoke directly to her brother.

"We can't find the words to express our feelings for you, Doug. We miss you. We wonder if there just might be a chance you'll come back. We pray for new vision and hope in the midst of our pain."

The number of searchers swelled again the day after the memorial. The RCMP put helicopters in the sky and boats in the nearby Peace River.

Cooper soon returned to business amidst the disturbed town and police investigation. Officers didn't have to worry about where he was. He reopened his clinic and began to see patients a week after the memorial.

Cooper refused every interview request from police. It was his constitutional right, he told them. Cooper didn't open his door to the reporters who knocked each day, either.

On May 23, the search for Snider was called off altogether.

Four days later, the police came for Cooper. They arrested him outside Fairview, in nearby Grande Prairie, while he worked at another clinic for the day. He was charged with first-degree murder. Two judges would later deny him bail.

In September 2000, Cooper's jury trial began in Edmonton because no one believed he would get a fair trial in northwest Alberta. A local juror who hadn't heard of Cooper would be impossible to find.

Crown prosecutors had boxes of evidence. The blood on Cooper's clothes and in his trunk was proven to be Snider's. The Nissan's trunk latch and the driver's floor mat supplied more blood.

Cooper's receptionist, Brenda Osowetski, saw blood on the floor of Cooper's clinic the morning after Snider disappeared. Cooper had an obvious motive. He wanted revenge.

Cooper's lawyer told the jury all that evidence could be explained. It was easy, said Larry Anderson. It was all fake. Snider was still alive, had staged his own death and planted his own blood to frame Cooper, Anderson said the day the trial opened. The missing doctor then callously left his family and practice behind, the jury heard.

Cooper was "set up," Cooper's lawyer claimed.

Anderson pointed to the key piece of evidence. The envelope Cooper gave his wife in the airport parking lot contained a letter that detailed Snider's guilt in Cooper's lawsuit. In ordered points and legal terms, Snider wrote that he actively conspired against Cooper. An expert determined Snider himself signed the letter. Cooper signed as a witness. It was typed on Cooper's office typewriter.

Prosecutors told the court Snider would never have signed his name voluntarily. It went against everything he'd told anyone about his situation with Cooper.

The jury and reporters heard thirty-eight witnesses. Some of them testified Cooper was a rough, honest man who'd only wanted to improve the Fairview Health Complex. Others described a man who spoke of using an axe handle to solve his lawsuit problem. His friends even gave him one.

The jury deliberated three days before they found Cooper guilty of the lesser charge of manslaughter in October 2000. After the time he'd already spent in jail, there was another seven years and four months to serve.

Cooper stood at his sentencing hearing and insisted Snider was still alive. Cooper's own private detective told him so, he said.

"I'm completely confident that within one year I will know the whereabouts of Dr. Snider, and when I have that information, I will share it with the press."

In the court gallery, some people gasped. Others laughed.

Snider's body has not been found.

PIPELINE

In January 2010, the RCMP had what they needed to raid the Trickle Creek compound in northwestern Alberta. A Grande Prairie judge had signed a five-day search warrant. Hopefully, five would be enough. The isolated property was huge, home to more than fifty people, and sprawled over seven hundred and fifty acres dotted with homes, sheds, barns, greenhouses, and mechanical shops. The compound was a community. Several families birthed children on the property and educated them at home as they grew older. Off the farm, the Ludwig family that led Trickle Creek ran a drywalling business among the towns in northwestern Alberta.

Nearly one hundred officers, including a heavily armed Emergency Response Team, were scheduled to help. Perhaps there wouldn't be any trouble at the gate. Perhaps there would. Police believed there were guns at Trickle Creek.

All the details were planned except one. What to do with Wiebo?

The sixty-eight-year-old Wiebo Ludwig was known to every police officer in the province. The wide man with a large shock of white hair and even larger beard was a long-time aggressive environmental activist. Loud and charismatic, Ludwig railed against the sour gas wells near Trickle Creek that caused miscarriages and serious health problems among his large family. Oil companies didn't give a damn about public health, he'd often argued. He'd once posed with a rifle in his hands for the cover of a book about him.

Ludwig's anger couldn't always be curbed by the law. In 2001, he was released from a nine-month stint in jail after he bombed and vandalized oil patches in Alberta. Now, nine years later, there had been six bomb attacks on pipelines owned by oil giant EnCana around Dawson Creek, British Columbia, seventy-four kilometres northwest of Trickle Creek. The police called it domestic terrorism.

Officers didn't want Ludwig, the main authority at Trickle Creek, to be present when they arrived. Ludwig was a mischievous and rebellious figure to some Albertans, but that didn't make him safe.

Days before, officers phoned the Ludwigs to discuss an offer Wiebo made to act as an intermediary between police and the unknown bomber. A meeting was scheduled at a Grande Prairie hotel on the morning of January 7. Such meetings were nothing new for Ludwig and local RCMP officers. Some of the invitations came from Ludwig and others from the police. They approached him several times for insight into who was bombing the EnCana properties.

Wiebo Ludwig and his son Josh drove the sixty kilometres into Grande Prairie early on a cold Friday morning. Josh was backing his pickup into a parking space at the Super 8 Hotel when an RCMP cruiser screeched to a stop at his front bumper and blocked their exit. Ten police officers converged around the truck from between parked cars.

Get out, one of them screamed.

The Ludwigs got out.

Officers arrested Wiebo and frisked him in the parking lot. Other officers pulled Josh Ludwig into one of the Super 8 rooms and locked the door.

Immediately, Josh asked to call the compound. Not a chance, police officers said.

At 8:00 a.m., with Wiebo in custody and Josh trapped in a hotel room, the RCMP search party arrived at the gates of Trickle Creek.

* * *

The EnCana bombings had begun with a letter several months earlier, in October 2008. Newspapers in a small patch of northeastern British Columbia, including the towns of Tom's Lake and Dawson Creek, received an unsigned letter printed in a rough hand.

. "To EnCana and all other oil and gas interests in the Tom's Lake area, you have until Oct. 11 of 2008 (Saturday 12 noon) to close down your operation (including the Steep Rock plant) and leave the area until further notice.

"We will not negotiate with terrorists which you are as you keep on endangering our families with crazy expansion of deadly gas wells in our home lands."

The day after the letter arrived, a bomb exploded at a natural gas pipeline east of Dawson Creek. The blast nearly breached the twelve-inch diameter steel pipe. There were enough explosives to hollow a two-metre hole where the pipe came above ground. The bombing site was so remote that a wandering hunter discovered the damage.

The RCMP brought in national security investigators hours later.

That same week, a second bomb exploded on the pipeline twenty kilometres from the first. The explosion spread debris over three hundred metres of snow and dead grass. In the morning, two electricians arrived at the site unaware and heard a loud hiss as toxic hydrogen sulphide leaked into the air.

The second blast stirred up fear and anger among the community not seen with the first. Though the leak wasn't serious enough for an evacuation, the thirty nearest residents were put on a health alert while the pipe was fixed. Tate Creek Elementary School in Tom's Lake was forced into emergency lockdown as students worked without lights or heat.

Two hundred residents of Tom's Lake held an angry meeting in the school gymnasium and demanded answers from the RCMP. Residents began to suspect the constant stream of truckers in the isolated corner of British Columbia.

"What do we do now?" resident Bobbie-Ann Weipert yelled at the meeting. "Just go home and sleep tight?"

The third bomb went off on Halloween. This time, a wellhead was damaged and another small leak occurred.

Then, for the next two months, there was nothing. No explosions, no sabotage.

Investigators released surveillance photos of people who mailed letters from the Shoppers Drug Mart in Dawson Creek before the bomber's notes arrived. Chemical experts analyzed the remaining traces of the bombs. Police asked for DNA samples from anyone who'd loudly voiced opposition to projects like the sour gas pipeline. RCMP helicopters flew overhead each day. EnCana security guards stopped traffic and talked to drivers. They knocked on doors and asked more questions.

Widespread suspicion festered in the area. People wondered if it was someone they knew, someone who lived on their street. For the culprit to be so angry, most agreed, he or she must be local. Many residents discussed their theories, and everyone listened. Though no one supported the bomber aloud, many thought little of the rampant oil and gas exploration that surrounded them. Still, neither gossip nor the investigation led anywhere. By late December, the RCMP investigation ran out of leads and ground to a halt.

On January 4, a fourth explosion blew out the side of an EnCana shed over a section of pipe across a country road from the home of a family with two children.

Days later, EnCana posted a $500,000 reward for information that led to the bomber. A flurry of tips followed, but no arrests.

Six quiet months then stretched by as police worked to find a criminal who had apparently quit. People breathed easier in Tom's Lake and Dawson Creek. It was a peaceful spring, and summer was ahead.

Ten minutes before the Canada Day parade in Dawson Creek, an RCMP officer tapped Mayor Mike Bernier on the shoulder and told him there'd been another explosion. This one was closer than the others, only five kilometres from town. Bernier smiled and waved for the sake of the parade even as he felt sick inside.

The bomber struck the pipeline again four days later.

A second hand-printed letter arrived at the front desk of the *Dawson Creek Daily News* two weeks later. The author gave EnCana five years to pack up everything and get out of northeastern British Columbia.

"Cease all your activities and remove all your installations. Return the land to what it was before you came, every last bit of it," the letter stated, "before things get a lot worse for you and your terrorist pals in the oil and gas business.

"You have three months to convince the residents here and the general public that you will commit to this program meaning that all actions against you will cease for three months from the time of this note. We can all take a summer vacation including your security personnel and the RCMP who have not helped you to date anyway—which was the whole point of the six minor and fully controlled explosions: to let you know that you are indeed vulnerable, can be rendered helpless despite your megafunds, your political influence, craftiness, and deceit in which you trusted."

EnCana raised its reward to $1 million. Behind closed doors, the company knew the attacks had already cost them $8 million in repairs and lost production.

The bomber held the three-month truce. In the midst of it, Wiebo Ludwig sent an open letter to newspapers that called on the bomber to stop. Still, he couldn't hide his admiration.

"You need to know that you have already set a lot of good things in motion," Ludwig wrote.

It was no surprise Ludwig involved himself. Anyone with an interest in the case had thought of him in his compound an hour's drive from the bombing sites.

Reporters asked police about Ludwig's possible involvement.

"It's something that we will be examining," Sergeant Tim Shields said.

* * *

In Alberta, he'd been a well-known character for years. Perfect strangers called him Wiebo, and everyone knew who they meant. Some thought of him as an eco-terrorist, others an eco-warrior.

A former Ontario pastor in the Christian Reformed Church, Ludwig first came to public and police attention in the mid-1990s when vandals struck several sour gas wells around Trickle Creek. The compound was less populated then, with only half of the fifty people there when the RCMP arrived in 2010.

For years, Ludwig fought the sour gas wells around his farm within the law. He made phone calls, filled out paperwork, and lodged protests with the government. He told anyone who would listen that the wells poisoned his land, livestock, and family. Ludwig was determined, cunning, and accustomed to being followed. Still, his sole success was in keeping exploration off his own land.

In November 1997, Ludwig encased a wellhead in cement and set it ablaze. He left a $2-million invoice for the grief caused to the Ludwig family. He even brought a videotape of the wrecked well to a television station the next day.

Over the years, the animosity between Ludwig and the RCMP, the oil companies, and eventually the general public grew bitter and personal. The Mounties created a task force at a cost of $750,000 to investigate his vandalism, which continued for more than a year.

On August 21, 1998, Wiebo's grandson Abel Ryan was stillborn with a deformed, soft skull. The family blamed the sour gas wells surrounding their property. They said such defects had been caused before in both humans and animals. Two nights later, Ludwig blew up an oil well sixty kilometres north of Hinton, at the edge of the Rocky Mountains. He was arrested the next day.

Ludwig was convicted of his vandalism spree in April 2000.

The RCMP did not escape unscathed from the battle with Ludwig. The conviction was surrounded by criticism of the police for a perceived closeness with the oil companies. Investigators blew up a well shack so an informant could gain credibility with Trickle Creek. Most of that informant's testimony was invalidated in court because the RCMP used a broken tape recorder.

The worst moment of the tension between the Ludwigs and their neighbours came on the night of June 20, 1999, less than a year before Wiebo went to jail. Karman Willis, a local sixteen-year-old, was shot dead as she and her and friends were joyriding in a truck on Trickle Creek's property. RCMP believed they found the rifle that killed Karman on the compound, but could never prove who pulled the trigger.

No one was ever charged with Karman's death.

* * *

With Wiebo in custody and Josh in a hotel room, the rest of the family and Richard Boonstra, Ludwig's right-hand man, greeted the officers who arrived at Trickle Creek. The officers wanted to force all the residents onto buses and put them into hotels for five days.

Boonstra rejected the idea outright. "This is our home. This is our property. You're hounds of the industry."

The majority of Trickle Creek stayed put while Wiebo's wife, Mamie, went to her husband in Grande Prairie. Anyone from Trickle Creek needed a police escort to leave, as officers blocked the roads three kilometres away. There were always thirty police officers on the compound as they searched in around-the-clock shifts. They confined the residents to certain buildings while they searched others.

"They're all over the place," observed Ben Ludwig, one of Wiebo's sons.

In Grande Prairie, officers told Wiebo they would charge him with extortion for the threatening EnCana letters.

"If I were you, I'd suspect me," Ludwig told them. He didn't say much else.

After a daylong, marathon interrogation, RCMP let Ludwig walk out the front door without charge and followed him home. Trickle Creek's patriarch rejoined his family to watch police search his home. The unflappable Ludwig calmly spoke to reporters on the phone as he watched officers turn his life upside down. He chastised those same reporters for paying attention to him instead of environmental concerns. Still, Ludwig didn't try hard to get off the phone.

The warrant stated that officers were looking for pens, paper, stationery, stamps, videos, computers, computer parts, boots, and dynamite—anything needed to write the letters or build the bombs. Officers carted away a fax machine and a number of computers. They took office supplies, chemistry textbooks, a crossbow, and a broken shotgun.

The task force secured a court order to sample Ludwig's DNA and took that too. Police already had Wiebo's DNA from a T-shirt and napkin obtained during an investigation a decade before. They already knew that DNA matched evidence taken from the EnCana letter envelopes.

Ludwig denied it all. It was possible his DNA was on the envelopes, but that didn't prove guilt, he told a reporter while he ate a cheeseburger at the Grande Prairie A&W.

"There may have been some indirect contamination of my DNA. I may have been in the presence of someone who used the envelope. They say a handshake can do it. Those cops treated me like a pincushion, putting everything on me."

Two years later, at seventy, Wiebo Ludwig died of cancer at Trickle Creek.

POLITICAL SUICIDE

Pete Parrott was a good neighbour. On a Sunday morning in June 1956, he drove six kilometres to the Clark farm to offer the family his help milking their thirty dairy cows and feeding their sixty other cattle. George Anderson, the Clarks' hired hand, had visited Parrott's farm the day before and mentioned he might spend the night in nearby Stettler, missing the morning chores.

Parrott also knew John Etter Clark, whom everyone called Jack, and his wife, Margaret, had just returned from a week-long trip to Saskatchewan. Clark, who represented the Social Credit Party, had been the member of the Legislative Assembly for the Stettler area since 1952 and easily won a second term the previous summer. He'd spent an exhausting week on the Saskatchewan campaign trail for Social Credit candidates in that province's general election. Parrott figured the Clarks could use help after his own chores were finished.

Clark's truck and car were parked in the driveway when Parrott arrived. There was no sign of the family when he walked around the farmyard and through the barn, which was strange. In addition to Clark, his wife, and the hired Anderson, there were usually three young daughters and a son scampering about the farm.

No one answered when Parrott knocked on the front door of the two-storey home. He peered through the wide windows at the front entrance and saw no one. Parrott was about to leave when he heard a small sound from inside the house. Suspicious, he tried the front door, which was unlocked, and went inside.

Anderson lay on the living room floor with blood across his face and pooled beneath him. It was his ragged breaths Parrott had heard from outside. The neighbour ventured further inside the home, to the bedroom where eight-year-old Jenna and her younger sisters, Ann and Linda, slept. The girls were laid side by side in their Sunday clothes with their seven-year-old brother, Ross. Their heads were bloodied just like Anderson's. Each of them had a bullet hole between their eyes.

"It was terrible," Parrott would later say.

There was no phone in the Clark home, so Parrott sped the five kilometres to the nearest farm in his truck. Clark's uncle owned that farm. He told Parrott that Clark had borrowed his .22-calibre rifle the day before.

A second neighbour arrived at the Clark farm as Parrott spoke to police. Lee Graham searched the yard and yelled, but no one responded. Graham, like Parrott, was concerned enough to go inside the house.

Graham found two more victims. Margaret, still clad in her nightgown, was dead in the upstairs master bedroom. In a guest room, twenty-year-old Bill Olah, a family friend and sailor on leave, had been shot while he slept. Like the Clark children, both had bullet holes in their foreheads.

There were no signs of a struggle, no lamps overturned, no broken glass on the floor. The family's breakfast, now long cold, was uneaten on the kitchen table.

Sickened, Graham went outside and met the returning Parrott in the driveway.

I didn't see Jack in the house, Graham said.

Neither had Parrott.

Anderson died on the living room floor before help could arrive. Linda, the youngest child, died on the way to the hospital in Stettler. Seven people dead, and Jack Clark wasn't there.

Clark was a popular man in the area who, at forty-one, had already won two elections by wide margins. He'd grown up around Stettler and worked as a schoolteacher before entering politics. He'd married Margaret in 1947, and there were four children over the next nine years. A striking man with a square jaw and high forehead, Clark was a long-time member of the Central Alberta Dairy Pool, the Stettler Credit Union, and the Stettler Co-op. Everyone who lived there knew him.

Still, townspeople traded rumours and whispered stories amongst themselves. Clark was a psychiatric patient at Calgary's General Hospital several years before, people said. He broke down during a speech at the Legislature in Edmonton and had to come home to rest.

"I wouldn't have loaned him a gun, myself," Parrott told a newspaper reporter.

Neighbours noticed Clark had been sullen because his thousand-acre farm had recently suffered several financial setbacks. The local dairy co-operative refused to buy the farm's milk. His truck and farm equipment all needed repairs. About two-thirds of his property was already leased to other farmers.

"I have a good mind to go swimming in the lake and never stop," he told one neighbour. Buffalo Lake was only a twenty-minute walk from the farm.

RCMP officers and the press crowded the farm's driveway later that morning. Inspector Maurice Laberge found blood on the ground outside the home. The chores were done, which led police to believe Anderson was shot outside and dragged into the house. Some of the bodies had black powder marks around their wounds, which indicated the rifle barrel was pressed directly against their foreheads.

The search for Clark began an hour after officers arrived. They brought in underwater dragging equipment to search Buffalo Lake. RCMP officers secured a military plane from Penhold to scour the hilly fields surrounding the farm. Officers came from Wetaskiwin, Red Deer, and

Camrose. Neighbours loaned their horses so officers could search faster.

"All we know is we are searching for Mr. Clark," Laberge told reporters desperate for details. "We would just like to find him."

A description of Clark was called over the RCMP radios: "Armed and possibly mental."

Laberge noted that the rifle used in the killings was not yet found.

Mrs. Anderson, who'd known Clark since he was a kid, drove from Stettler to the farm when she heard the news. She remembered the childhood day he nearly drowned in Buffalo Lake and his fear of the water ever since. He never did learn to swim.

"I just can't understand it. I know Jack had been in off-health but it just doesn't make sense.

"Jack just treasured little Ann," Anderson added. "I hope he isn't alive."

Officers found no trace of Clark the first day.

Scared neighbours took their families into the safety of Stettler to spend the night. Those who stayed home didn't sleep.

It was the officers in the Otter airplane two hundred feet over the farm who spotted Jack Clark, thirty-one hours after the search began.

They found him face down in three feet of water in a slough close enough to be seen from his own kitchen window. He still wore his pyjamas, and the .22 rifle was nearby. As he had done to the others, Clark had put a bullet in his forehead.

GUILTY CONSCIENCE

When Leslie Charles Brown stumbled into the North Vancouver RCMP detachment in April 1988, he was a shell of the man he'd been six years before. Gaunt, rough, and ravaged by guilt, he was no longer recognizable as the Calgary family man he once was.

My wife is dead, he told police. I buried her in a refrigerator in Saskatchewan and I'm here to give myself up.

At first, officers thought Leslie was a misguided, drunk, homeless man with a tall tale. He certainly looked like one. The longer Leslie kept talking, the more details he revealed. The officers began to change their minds. If he was lying, he'd put a lot of thought into it.

"I just had to get it off my chest," the emaciated fifty-year-old Leslie told police. "I just want to do my penance."

RCMP called the Calgary Police Service and asked if they had a missing person file on a woman named Wilma Yupin Brown. They did, though there was hardly anything in it, even after six years.

The thirty-eight-year-old wife and mother of two was last seen in her northwest Calgary home in the early morning of March 25, 1982. Wilma, Leslie, and their sons were scheduled to fly to Trinidad to visit her relatives. It had been years since Wilma went home, and she was excited for the trip. In addition to the family's luggage, she'd packed another bag full of Canadian gifts for her parents. The day derailed quickly. At 7:30 a.m., one of the couple's sons called Leslie at work to say they couldn't find their mother.

Wilma had planned to help the boys with final preparations for their trip, but still wasn't there after Leslie hurried home. She wasn't at the neighbour's, at work, or anywhere else Leslie could think to call. It didn't make sense. Wilma was a loving mother to her boys and a devout Catholic who wouldn't walk away from a sixteen-year marriage friends and family swore was happy. It was even more perplexing that she vanished only hours before a planned reunion with her family in Trinidad.

"My reaction was one of puzzlement," neighbour Kevin Murphy would later testify. "It seemed so out of character for Wilma to just disappear."

That day, Leslie did everything a frantic husband would do. He reported his wife's disappearance to police and spent hours on the phone with neighbours, friends, and family in search of clues. No one could provide any answers. Her co-workers at the Bank of Nova Scotia, where she worked as a loans manager, were also stumped. Wilma's relatives in Port of Spain, Trinidad's capital, still expected the Brown family's arrival until they heard Wilma was missing.

Police soon confirmed Wilma's airline ticket was never cashed, adjusted, or used. Her clothes were still packed in her suitcase next to the bag of gifts for her family. Nothing was missing from the bedroom she shared with Leslie. If Wilma had run off, she hadn't taken her passport.

Investigators found no signs of a fight, no whispers of a secret life. As odd as her disappearance seemed, police found nothing incriminating. Leads were rare, and were mostly dead ends. Six weeks after her disappearance, a rumour surfaced that she was seen in Port of Spain, but neither her American brother nor Leslie found anything after weeks scouring the streets and asking questions on the small Caribbean island. Wilma was listed as a missing person with international police agency Interpol, but nothing came of it.

Within six months of Wilma's disappearance, Leslie moved his two sons to Vancouver. Perhaps your mother has been taken by a cult, he told them. Perhaps she fled the family because a book she'd recently read, *Flowers in the Attic*, brought back memories of a troubled childhood in Trinidad. The boys were too young to know how ridiculous their father's suggestions were.

It was all lies. Leslie knew exactly what had happened to his wife.

On the night before their trip to Trinidad, the Browns were fighting in their bedroom. Wilma told Leslie she was leaving him, and planned to stay in Trinidad. A violent argument erupted, and Leslie shoved his wife backwards. She tumbled into a chair, toppled over, and hit her head. Wilma was still crying on the floor when Leslie went to bed angry and fell asleep.

Four hours later, when Leslie woke, Wilma was dead under the covers beside him. There was blood on her pillow. Leslie panicked.

Quietly, he carried his wife's body past their sons' rooms and stashed her behind the basement stairs. He then showered, dressed, and went to work as though nothing was wrong. When his son phoned to say Wilma was missing, Leslie began his performance as the shocked, grieving husband. He played the role well, and officers inside the Brown home never suspected Wilma's body was right beneath their feet the whole time.

Days later, Leslie dragged Wilma's body from behind the stairs and wrapped her in plastic tarp and wire. He shoved her into an old refrigerator in the basement and secured the door with thick rope. Leslie brought the fridge upstairs with the help of an unknowing neighbour and slid the appliance into the box of his truck.

For three months, he kept the fridge in a Calgary storage unit while he faked a search for his wife and wondered how to dispose of her body. His solution was a vacation. After telling friends his sons needed time away, Leslie took them on a road trip to his mother's farm near Shellbrook, Saskatchewan, west of Prince Albert. One night, Leslie snuck away from his mother's house and buried the fridge on a forgotten corner of her property. He told his sons they had brought the fridge for a delivery in Saskatchewan.

Three months later, Leslie was in a downward spiral. As his sons grew into men, Leslie drank. His appetite was poor, and the weight dropped off him. Eventually, his alcoholism cost him his job. He was later kicked out of his apartment and landed on Vancouver's skid row in the downtown eastside.

Having reached rock bottom, Leslie walked into the North Vancouver RCMP detachment and confessed. His wife's case was long closed, and he'd never fallen under suspicion from anyone.

"I wanted to hide it from the kids," he told an officer. "I didn't want them to know that their daddy killed their mom. I didn't mean to kill her. I didn't even mean to hurt her."

Two days later, Leslie led Calgary homicide detectives to an isolated, overgrown patch of land on his mother's farm near Shellbrook. The rusted remains of a car were parked nearby.

Detective Wayne Lauinger handed Leslie a shovel and told him to dig.

"He hit the fridge with his first strike. It was only a few inches down under the surface," the officer remembered.

Wilma's bones were the only thing they found inside the fridge. Pathologists could never determine how she died.

Back in Calgary to face charges, Leslie confessed to his sons that he'd lied to them every day.

"He had said he was doing it for my brother and I, so he could raise us and let us grow up," Leslie Brown Jr., then twenty-two, told the court at his father's trial. "He believed it was more or less an accident."

In November 1989, Leslie was convicted of manslaughter and interfering with a dead body.

Court of Queen's Bench Justice Russell Dixon wondered aloud if Leslie created his lies to save himself, rather than his sons. The judge doubted Leslie was honest about how hard he shoved his wife the night she died.

"There are no circumstances that can be said to justify your bizarre actions in containing, storing, and transporting the remains of your wife," Dixon added.

HOCKEY BAG

For hours, Donna Parkinson quietly obsessed about the hockey bag her brother had left inside her garage. Earlier that day, their mother, Emily, brought her younger brother, Thomas Svekla—Donna and her sisters called him Tommy—to her Fort Saskatchewan bungalow for a visit. It was the first time she'd seen him since he was released from prison earlier that month, in May 2006. He'd served four months for breaching his bail conditions.

That was Tommy, always getting into trouble. There was the time he crashed into three cars in a stolen Buick and tried to flee. There was his drug-fuelled life in the northern town of High Level. There were the repeated charges of sexual assault against women who drifted in and out of his life while he was a mechanic at Fountain Tire. When he was thirty-six, he sexually abused his girlfriend's daughter. Later that year, he stumbled over the body of a woman named Rachel Quinney in the woods northeast of Edmonton. He told the police he was in the isolated area to smoke crack with a prostitute. That was Tommy.

Donna's heart pounded in her chest all afternoon. Her little brother scared her. When Tommy and her mother stepped out to run an errand, Donna went into her garage and quickly felt around the heavy, full hockey bag her brother had shoved into the back of her truck. Tommy claimed the bag was full of $800 worth of compost worms a friend gave him to transport.

Donna didn't believe it. Who would give someone fresh out of jail so many worms to transport from High Level to Edmonton? It made no sense, even for Tommy.

She swore she felt the point of an elbow inside the bag.

Donna took a deep breath and tried to stay calm when her brother and mother returned. Tommy wanted to take his young nephew to the park. Donna went with them.

"There was no hope in hell he was going to the park with my kid," she said later.

After her balding, smirking brother finally left with their mother for the night, Donna put her young son to bed. The hockey bag was still in her garage. When Jim Parkinson got home shortly before midnight, his wife was waiting for him on their driveway. As she stood bathed in the glow of headlights, Jim noticed Donna's work gloves.

"We're going in," Donna told him. "I want to know what is in that bag."

The couple pulled open the long zipper. There was something inside, wrapped in wire, layers of plastic, and a deflated air mattress the colour of dried mustard. It wasn't worms. Jim didn't know what it was.

"Do you not see what I see?" Donna asked her husband. "That is the head. These are the hands, these are the knees, and these are her feet."

* * *

Theresa Innes had officially been missing for two months, though it was at least five since anyone in High Level was certain they'd seen her. She was easy to lose track of. At thirty-six, her best years were already behind her. Her loving, six-year marriage had crumbled under the weight of drug addiction. Theresa was once full of life and described as "bubbly" by those who knew her best, but the drugs stole most of her spark. After her marriage fell apart, she drifted east from Nanaimo into Alberta, and ended up in the rough, isolated town of High Level where crack cocaine, Theresa's drug of choice, was easy to get.

Her addiction eventually outlasted her finances and she resorted to prostitution, a popular trade in a town surrounded by isolated work camps full of well-paid men with money. With fewer police, smaller towns like High Level drew sex-trade workers from across the province.

Theresa worked High Level's small bar district, jokingly called Vegas of the North because many hotels there were named after famous casinos on the Strip. She moved from bar to bar, drinking nothing stronger than coffee and soliciting the drunk patrons at their tables. Men liked that Theresa was friendly and kind. She soon lost track of her old life. Her family rarely heard from her. When she disappeared from her usual High Level haunts, people assumed she'd just left town.

* * *

By the time Donna called the police about her brother and his hockey bag, dead sex-trade workers had become dreadfully common around Edmonton. Authorities counted thirteen between 1988 and 2006. Many were found in fields northeast of the city, usually after the spring melt.

In October 2003, three years before Svekla's arrest, RCMP formed the Project Kare task force to investigate the murders and disappearances of women who lived "high-risk lifestyles." Across northern Alberta, people knew what that meant. They read the newspaper headlines and saw pictures of the victims on TV, mug shots of faces roughened by drug abuse and hard living.

Along Edmonton's 118th Avenue, known as the Avenue of Champions, women worked their street corners in fear. Drug-addled and skinny, they regularly got into cars with strange, unknown men. On 118th, business started at six o'clock in the morning when johns stopped on their way to work. All the women grieved at least one friend found dead. They recognized the faces staring out from newspaper boxes as they awaited their next trick.

Detective Jim Morrissey of Edmonton's vice squad spent many nights on the Avenue of Champions. It was not a nice place to be.

"This is not *Pretty Woman*," Morrissey told a newspaper reporter.

Morrissey and other detectives turned a blind eye to the prostitution. They couldn't protect women who were afraid of getting busted. To police, it was more important to document the girls than to make a few arrests. Detectives collected names, photographs, and strands of hair for DNA in case they disappeared. If they wouldn't leave the streets, police reasoned, at least they were documented. Should another go missing, there would be a picture to release to the public. Officers wanted reports on missing women as soon as they vanished.

Police believed the killer was a frequent john, a man they would recognize when they caught him.

"It's someone we know," Morrissey said.

The day after he left Theresa Innes in his sister's garage, forty-year-old Thomas Svekla became Project Kare's first arrest. Police charged him with her murder, and later, with the killing of nineteen-year-old Rachel Quinney, the woman whose body he claimed to have stumbled over in the woods outside Edmonton.

Svekla was acquitted of Quinney's murder the same day he was convicted of killing Innes.

Svekla was proud of his infamy in the Edmonton Remand Centre, where fellow inmates called him Hockey Bag, and the Pickton of Alberta, a reference to infamous British Columbia pig farmer Robert Pickton, who was convicted for the murder of six Vancouver sex-trade workers in 2009.

Svekla held no anger toward the sister who turned him in.

"Donna, you did good," he told her on the phone from prison. "You did the right thing."

SNATCHED FROM SCHOOL

On a crisp afternoon in March of 1981, inside the washroom at St. Elizabeth Catholic School in southeast Edmonton, six-year-old Kevin Alarie was washing a cut on his arm. The first-grade student had fallen and scraped himself on the playground during recess. He was standing at the row of sinks when he spotted a startling reflection in the mirror. A tall man in dark clothing emerged from a stall behind him and quickly clamped his hand over Kevin's mouth.

The intruder then carried Kevin, kicking and squirming, out of the washroom, down the empty corridor, and outside to a waiting car. His teenaged male accomplice sat behind the wheel wearing a dress so the pair would appear at first glance to be parents of a student. Kevin's abductor shoved the terrified little boy into the back seat as the car sped away from the school and through the surrounding Mill Woods neighbourhood. No one from the school noticed Kevin was missing until after the car was long gone. All the other kids were on the other side of the schoolyard for recess.

"We need your phone number and address," the tall man said as the captors drove the boy downtown. Then they told him to keep quiet and stay on the floor of the car.

A half-hour later, at two o'clock, staff at St. Elizabeth's realized Kevin was gone. Teachers and older students found no sign of him during a quick search of the school grounds. His jacket and empty lunchbox were still on the hooks in the hall where he'd left them. Teachers knew the gap-toothed Kevin as a quiet student who never caused trouble. It made little sense for him to run off. If he had, why wouldn't he wear his jacket? It wasn't warm enough for just shirt sleeves that early spring day.

School staff called police and then Kevin's mother, Sandra Alarie. Her husband, Gilbert, rushed home from work.

Through the late afternoon, police told the frantic parents the simplest explanation was the most likely—Kevin had wandered off and become lost.

Just after 5:00 p.m., investigators gave a description of the skinny boy to radio and television stations for broadcast on the six o'clock news. He's missing his front left tooth, reporters were told, and has short, messy brown hair and brown eyes.

Ten minutes later, Sandra excused herself from a conversation with investigators to answer the phone in her kitchen.

"Shut up and listen," an excited and high-pitched voice told her. "We've got your kid. If you want to see him again, you've got three days to raise a hundred thousand dollars. Don't call the police 'cause we're watching your place. If you don't do what we want, we'll ship your kid back to you in pieces."

The line went dead. Sandra fell to the floor in tears.

Immediately, police called the media back and told them not to put Kevin's description out to the public. They didn't say why. Reporters assumed an innocently lost boy had been found unharmed.

Inspector Fred Allan, a twenty-eight-year police veteran, was assigned to lead the investigation of the first child kidnapping for ransom in Edmonton's history. A child taken right out of his own school. Parents across the city were going to lose their minds.

In a crooked, ramshackle boarding house on 107A Avenue near the downtown core, Rennie Ronald Sookram hung up the phone. His plan had gone perfectly since he'd grabbed the kid in the washroom that morning. The twenty-one-year-old had tossed Kevin on an old couch when they got inside the second-floor suite.

"Lay down on the couch and be quiet," he told the boy. Kevin listened. Sookram and his partners gave him a glass of milk and a bowl of popcorn. On the suite's small television, Wile E. Coyote chased The Road Runner along the edge of a deep canyon.

Sookram was an ambitious young criminal, but lacked experience. He'd moved to Canada from the Caribbean republic of Trinidad and Tobago when he was nine. He was the youngest in a family of five that went through divorce when he was a teen. Following a troubled youth in Winnipeg, he'd moved to Edmonton ten months before with plans to start his own criminal organization.

On the street, Sookram was known as Serpico. He either didn't know or didn't care that the name was inspired by Frank Serpico, an honest cop from New York played by Al Pacino in a movie nine years before. Few criminals adopted the names of famous police officers.

Sookram badly wanted to move up in the world. He needed the hundred grand as start-up cash to form a drug-dealing crew that would include his four accomplices in the kidnapping. They were all his age or younger, including the sixteen-year-old wheelman who'd worn a dress that afternoon. Sookram already knew which of his friends he would choose for specific roles in his drug operation and had planned to kidnap a kid for almost two months. In his mind, committing a major crime was the smartest way to get the cash to fund minor ones.

Sookram needed a kid with rich parents. He assumed Kevin's were. He chose St. Elizabeth specifically because all the students were from Mill Woods families. Surely any of them could afford a hundred grand, Sookram thought, with the big houses they lived in. Any child from the school would have worked. Sookram didn't even know Kevin's name until they were already making their getaway.

Some of the ransom payment would have to go to a new place. The boarding suite was a dump, not even worth the

$140 rent. Bare bulbs were strung across the water-stained ceiling, and the wallpaper was an ugly floral pattern. The previous tenant had hung maps of the Northwest Territories in all three rooms.

Sookram was confident the money would come through. After he had his cash, they would inject Kevin full of morphine and send him home in a taxi. If the parents refused to pay, they could always throw the kid in the North Saskatchewan River, Sookram told his friends.

The plan didn't include any more calls to the Alarie home until the next day. That Tuesday night, Kevin slept under the living room table, with a sheet hung over it to hide him. His captors tossed thin blankets on the dirty floor for the boy to sleep on.

I want to go home, Kevin pleaded.

You have to stay, Sookram told him.

No one slept at the Alarie house. Police officers were in the house through the night. They wore plain clothes and kept their cruisers away from the street outside. On Allan's order, the family phone was now wiretapped.

On Wednesday morning, police chief Robert Lunney held an off-the-record meeting with representatives of Edmonton's newspapers and television stations. He wanted to keep news of the kidnapped child under wraps and knew word would eventually leak if he didn't step in. Lunney told the editors and producers Kevin's life would be in greater jeopardy if they covered the story. The kidnappers would see the coverage, realize police must be involved, and then do God knows what. The media agreed when Lunney promised they would get more off-the-record updates.

Shortly after noon on Wednesday, Sandra received another phone call from the men who stole her boy. They would only speak with her. The call seemed to have no purpose other than to torture the harrowed mother. Sookram refused to let Sandra speak with Kevin or even offer her proof he was still alive. The line went dead after Sookram threatened to cut off Kevin's fingers with a hunting knife. The officers in the Alarie kitchen all checked their watches in frustration. They needed a phone call to last more than three minutes to get a trace. That one hadn't even been close.

Sookram didn't call again until after midnight. As detectives listened, Sandra told him the $100,000 was ready. Police had collected the cash from banks, wrapped the stacks of bills in rubber bands, and piled them neatly in a black briefcase on the Alarie kitchen table. Sookram demanded she bring the money to Fuller's Restaurant downtown, only four blocks from where Kevin slept under a table. Sookram told Sandra he would call later with a time.

At sunrise on Thursday morning, Sookram called back. Be at Fuller's at 11:15 this morning, he told her, then wait thirty minutes. Just her.

The second call was longer than three minutes and gave police the trace they were hoping for. It led to a downtown phone booth that was empty when officers arrived.

Gilbert drove his wife to the rendezvous at Fuller's Restaurant and waited nervously in the car. Inside, Sandra sat at a table with the black briefcase beside her while officers watched. Sandra stared at everyone who walked through the door, but no one came to her table. The thirty minutes passed. She waited another forty-five before she left.

The failed meeting only made things worse for the Alarie family. Why had the kidnappers not shown? Did they spot the police officers? Was Kevin still alive?

With no word, the afternoon passed excruciatingly slowly.

A little after four in the afternoon, Sookram called Sandra and ordered her back to Fuller's immediately. He was furious, but didn't explain why the morning meeting had failed. Again, Gilbert drove his wife downtown, and she went inside the restaurant with the briefcase. Again, no one showed. Sandra's nerves were shot.

Back at the Alarie home, Allan coached Sandra for the next phone call. He wanted her to be more aggressive and fight back against their insults and abuse. They would only speak to her, the mother, because they believed she was the most vulnerable, Allan said.

Sookram called again Thursday night. His crew of druggies had screwed up his disorganized plan, and everything had gone wrong once they all took turns watching Kevin and trying to collect the money. Sookram screamed over the line at Sandra. As Allan listened, Sandra yelled right back, antagonizing Sookram into a verbal confrontation. He repeatedly blamed her for the botched meetings at the restaurant, even though she'd done everything right.

Under the table in the rooming house, Kevin listened to Sookram's side of the conversation. At times, he could hear his mother's raised voice over the phone. The boy never knew his mother to sound so furious.

By the time Sookram hung up, it was too late. Sandra had drawn the call out longer than three minutes. Allan smiled.

Police traced the call to the rooming house at the northeast edge of downtown, but didn't go inside. Just because the kidnappers called from the house didn't necessarily mean Kevin was inside. A raid on the wrong house would only spook the kidnappers and show Allan's hand. Instead, they watched rough-looking people come and go from the house through Thursday night and into Friday morning.

The police tapped the phone in the rooming house and waited.

In the early afternoon, one of Sookram's crew made a careless phone call from the rooming house and casually mentioned to a friend there was "a kid in the closet." It was all police needed.

Fifteen minutes later, eight detectives were ready to storm the boarding house. The wooden building had two balconies recently hammered onto the back end next to a thin staircase. The phone police tapped was on the second floor, behind a window obscured by the reaching branches of a dead tree in the backyard.

Four detectives crept up the unsteady staircase as four others approached the front. They kicked in both doors simultaneously. Sookram and two of his crew were arrested in seconds.

Detective John Bakker had spent the past three days in the Alarie home. While his colleagues handcuffed the kidnappers, Bakker crouched and lifted the sheet covering the living room table.

"Hi Kevin, it's the police," Bakker said. "Come with me."

The unhurt boy leapt into the detective's arms, and Bakker walked outside. At police headquarters, doctors were examining Kevin when his parents burst into the room. Sandra and Gilbert smothered him in their arms without saying a word.

"Today has probably been the best day of my career as a policeman," Bakker said as he witnessed the reunion.

At police headquarters, investigators threw a small celebration for Kevin and invited the media, who had waited days to report the story. One of the officers gave the boy an oversized cowboy hat that swallowed the tops of his ears.

As his son sat on his lap, Gilbert Alarie felt like he'd gone through three days of hell.

"The waiting was murder. You don't know what it's like until you've been through something like this. After living in hell, it's nice to get out of it. I feel like five thousand pounds have been lifted off my shoulders."

Sandra barely let her son out of her arms in the hours after his rescue. Pictures of her cradling the weary and smiling Kevin were all over Edmonton the next day. "I still can't believe we got him back in one piece."

Allan had barely slept over the three days. The police inspector wore a smile on his face, but the eyes behind his large glasses were blurry and dragged down by dark circles.

"There were times when we had our fears and doubts. However, we always kept our hopes."

BURIED

For seventeen years, rumours swirled in Medicine Hat about the disappearance of Tadeus Gawron. The sixty-three-year-old was born in Poland and met his wife, Sofia, at the end of the Second World War in a Polish labour camp. Eventually, in the 1970s, the couple immigrated to Canada with their four children, and moved into a bungalow on Prospect Drive in Medicine Hat with a vegetable garden and flowers in the backyard. Tadeus, a stout man, walked to work at the Canadian Pacific Railway yard, while Sofia cultivated plants in one of Medicine Hat's many greenhouses.

The couple separated in 1980. Sofia kept the family home, and Tadeus vanished shortly thereafter. He didn't tell friends where he was going and left no word with his children. People in the southeast Alberta town simply stopped seeing him around.

Joe Marik, Gawron's boss at Canadian Pacific Railway until he retired in 1976, didn't believe Tadeus suddenly started a new life after his marriage fell apart. Marik's gut told him to be suspicious.

"He wouldn't have gone anywhere," Marik said. "I don't think he even owned a car. No one just disappears. We knew something had happened to him."

Members of the Medicine Hat Police Service questioned Gawron's friends, but found no reason to suspect foul play. If he chose to, a grown man was allowed to walk away from his life without a word.

Sofia attracted curious glances around town in the weeks after Tadeus was last seen. In one of her rare appearances in public, she sold her ex-husband's belongings in a massive garage sale. Small price tags were attached to everything from his fishing tackle to his bicycle. Neighbours wondered why he hadn't taken any of his belongings with him when he left town.

There was also the new seven-foot fence Sofia constructed around her small backyard. In all of Medicine Hat, there was no other fence as high and uninviting. It became the weirdest home in the neighbourhood the day the job was done.

"She put braces up and two rows of barbed wire," remembered Sara-Ann McMillan, the Gawrons' next-door neighbour. "It was just like the Berlin Wall."

It would be another seven years before Gawron was reported missing, when his son Kenneth went to the Medicine Hat Police Service and filed a report. No one in the family had heard from him. It was too long a time to be missing, even for a man whose decades-long marriage went sour. Police finally opened a file on the missing Polish senior in 1987.

That same year, the government discovered Sofia was committing fraud by cashing Canada Pension Plan and Canadian Pacific Railway benefits cheques addressed to Tadeus. He'd never given anyone a forwarding address.

Still, aside from his children's concern, there were no new leads in the case. Crucial years passed without any official investigation, and Gawron's file remained empty until 1991, when Kenneth Gawron had his father legally declared dead at the Medicine Hat courthouse. More than a decade without a phone call, letter, or sighting convinced Kenneth his father couldn't be alive.

Sofia eventually left Medicine Hat and moved west to Pincher Creek, on the eastern edge of the Rockies. Agnes Dennis, a fellow senior and Sofia's next-door neighbour, knew the quiet, reclusive woman with the thick Polish accent better than most. She was always worried people would jump her chain-link fence and steal vegetables from her garden. She didn't want anyone in her yard.

Sofia rarely mentioned Tadeus to Agnes, but spoke often of how she could never return to Medicine Hat. When Sofia complained about the harsh winds in Pincher Creek, Agnes asked her why she wouldn't move back.

"She said if she went back, something bad would happen," Agnes recalled. "She said she'd be blown away."

The missing person file gathered dust in the records of the Medicine Hat Police Department until January 1997, when officers received a tip from an anonymous caller who said Tadeus never actually left Medicine Hat alive. Officers reopened the file and began a quiet, five-month investigation. Medicine Hat's residents had no idea their small police department now believed Tadeus had met a violent end.

In June of 1997, a van full of men with coveralls and shovels pulled up to the home on Prospect Drive. By that time, the house had changed hands twice and the Berlin Wall fence was long gone. Both families that had lived in the Gawron house knew the whole bizarre story. New owners had renovated the home's interior and landscaped the yard. There were a slide and swing on the lawn.

The police investigation seemed more like routine gardening until workers dug up the backyard. Forensic experts watched carefully as uprooted plants and ragged sod piled up. The officers didn't have to dig too deep.

They found some of Tadeus Gawron under the garden. They found some of him beneath the lawn. His body had been cut into pieces and buried.

From her window, Patsy Walker watched as officers unearthed the one-man graveyard behind her home. The house had never made her uncomfortable, but now she was unnerved by the reporters and residents who slowly drove past with long stares and morbid curiosity once the news broke.

The bones were painstakingly exhumed and sent to the medical examiner's office in Calgary to determine how Tadeus died. In those offices, there was little for examiner Lloyd Denmark to work with.

"How can you tell if the man had a heart attack when he has no heart?" Denmark asked. "How can you tell if he was strangled if he has no neck?"

Police were quick to tell the media none of the Gawron children were suspects. They couldn't say the same for Sofia.

The seventy-nine-year-old now lived across the province in the mountain town of Blairmore. She'd been a patient in the long-term care ward of the Crowsnest Pass Health Care Centre for three years. All the seniors who lived in the centre were under long-term care for dementia, Alzheimer's, and other neurological conditions.

In August, Medicine Hat prosecutor Darwin Greaves asked officers to identify a toxic substance found in the soil around Gawron's bones. At the time, toxicology labs in Alberta didn't have the resources to pinpoint the substance.

Because Sofia worked for years in one of Medicine Hat's many greenhouses, Greaves theorized the chemical was some type of now-banned pesticide. It was bad stuff, as Greaves described it, the kind that would make a man glow in the dark. Perhaps Tadeus had been poisoned, the prosecutor considered.

Greaves seemed determined to solve the mystery.

"I've told the police, damn the cost," he informed reporters. "We're going to go wherever we can to get it analyzed, period. I said go elsewhere—wherever—I don't care how many labs you have to contact."

Greaves, however, had more theory than proof. Sofia was charged in October for improper treatment of a dead body, but not murder. She was also charged with fraud for collecting her husband's pension cheques for seven years.

Prosecutor Stephanie Cleary said the investigation failed to uncover how Gawron died.

"We do know, however, that before his death, Tadeus Gawron was a very, very sick man," she said.

Sofia missed her first court appearance because she was too frail to travel, her lawyer told a Medicine Hat judge. Soon after, prosecutors requested she undergo psychiatric tests to determine if she was fit to stand trial at all.

When the results came back, prosecutors didn't even try to argue with the conclusion that she wasn't mentally fit. In January, officers brought the white-haired Sofia into a Medicine Hat courtroom in a wheelchair. The judge halted the charges against her, and she returned to her hospital bed in Blairmore.

For many in Medicine Hat, a trial wasn't necessary to make up their minds. Sofia was guilty.

"There was always a lot of gossip, but we never dreamed our suspicions may have been true," Joe Marik said of his former employee's death.

GREASE MONKEY

As most of Stettler's residents sat in church, a pair of RCMP officers tried to tell Robert Cook's family they had him in their holding cell. It was hardly a surprise that the twenty-two-year-old Cook was in trouble. On that Sunday–June 28, 1959–Cook was only five days out of the Prince Albert Penitentiary. He'd been sentenced to three years for car theft and bank robbery, but released early because of an amnesty for non-violent offenders to mark a visit from Queen Elizabeth II. It was an efficient way to relieve the crowded Canadian prisons at the time and Cook benefited. He'd arrived in Stettler two days earlier to see his father, his stepmother, and their five young children.

This latest imprisonment was his first as an adult, but Cook had been in and out of juvenile prisons for years. His childhood took a wrong turn when he was nine and his mother died during a routine operation. A year later, his father married Cook's schoolteacher and moved the family to Stettler, a town of three thousand, east of Red Deer. A new half-brother or half-sister came every year after. By thirteen, he'd transformed his obsession with auto repair, a hobby he picked up from his father, into a string of stolen cars. At one point, he was involved with youth boxing in Stettler. Smaller than many of his opponents, Cook used to kick other kids when they fell in the ring.

Stettler RCMP had taken the stocky Cook into custody the previous afternoon. He'd been driving around town in a white Chevrolet Impala convertible, fresh from an Edmonton dealership that morning. He was showing off. The decorative streamers used by the dealership still hung from the car. An RCMP officer cornered him on Main Street and ordered he go to the detachment on his own, which he did. Stettler police had received a call from Edmonton about the Impala. Cook had apparently posed as his father and traded the family's Chevrolet station wagon for the convertible.

No one answered when police knocked on the Cooks' door that morning. Surrounded by thick hedges and a picket fence, officers waited near the green-and-white house on Railway Avenue. No one came home even after parishioners left church services. One neighbour told officers he'd called the Cook house Thursday night and Robert told him the family had gone to Vancouver on a holiday. Another neighbour who called was told they'd gone west to Hanna for a family visit. The children hadn't played in the yard for days.

The two officers had too many questions. They went through the front door.

Inside, the home was soaked red with blood. It was on the walls in the girls' bedroom on the main floor and the boys' in the basement. Streaks stained the beds of Cook's father and his half-siblings. It clung tacky to the shotgun the police found stuffed under a mattress. There was more blood in the small attached garage.

Years earlier, Cook's father had dug a six-foot pit to stand in while he repaired the underside of cars. The officers removed the wooden planks covering the hole, and a foul stench wafted from underground. The pit was filled with boxes, blankets, and bald tires. They rummaged deeper and found the bodies of Cook's father, Raymond, and his wife, Daisy. Beneath them, the bodies of the children—Gerald, Patrick, Christopher, Kathy, and Linda Mae—were still clad in their pyjamas. The adults were shot, then the shotgun had been turned around and used to bludgeon the children.

"It appears to be the work of a maniac," one officer said.

Back at the detachment, RCMP charged Cook with murder two hours after the bodies were found.

"You think it was me. You all do," Cook said. "I just didn't do it. That's all I've got in the world. What would you think I would want to hurt them for?"

The next day, Cook appeared in front of a judge who ordered him to the Ponoka Mental Hospital, ninety kilometres away, for a month-long observation.

* * *

Ten days later, Cook escaped.

There was no guard posted at his room. A hospital staff member checked on him every half-hour. In the time between checks, near midnight on July 10, Cook wrenched the steel mesh from his window and smashed his way outside, clad in a hospital robe and slippers.

Cook immediately fell back on familiar skills and stole a Ford Monarch from the parking lot. He sped out of Ponoka with a slight head start. Investigators found the black-and-white vehicle crashed in a ditch thirty kilometres outside of town. The only sign of Cook was a hospital slipper found inside the car.

RCMP were quick to label Cook "extremely dangerous" as the most extensive manhunt in Alberta's history began. A hundred police officers converged on the area between Ponoka and Red Deer. They brought in search dogs from all corners of the province. Many locals volunteered to search and were turned down. Police believed Cook, not yet convicted of mass murder, would not survive if hunted by armed citizens still shocked by the slaughter of his family. They didn't want to risk any vigilante justice.

Police knew it wouldn't be easy to find their fugitive. The area was crossed with plenty of escape routes and dotted with farms and forest. Cook grew up there, and was well acquainted with the lay of the land. Crazy for anything with an engine and a steering wheel, he knew every secondary road and dirt trail. Officers contacted owners of private planes to search from above and warned motorists not to pick up hitchhikers.

Fear spread when Cook was not captured immediately. Farmers locked their vehicles to squelch any temptation to steal a ride from their property. Families slept with rifles next to their beds, and farmers did their daily chores with loaded shotguns nearby. No one slept soundly for ten kilometres in all directions. Some farmers moved into the nearest town to feel safe. Other families stayed in each others' homes so they could sleep in shifts and keep more eyes on their children.

Newspaper headlines screamed of Cook's escape. The news pushed aside articles about the royal visit that freed him from prison in the first place.

Police found no trace of Cook until the next day, when someone discovered a piece of his striped hospital robe near the dance hall in the town of Alix, fifty-four kilometres southeast of Ponoka. Cook had broken into the hall and grabbed a loaf of bread and several bottles of soda. Nearby, another car had been stolen.

Inspector Maurice Laberge, the RCMP officer leading the manhunt, was frustrated. The area was full of roadblocks, crawling with police officers, and plastered with photos of Cook, yet somehow he slipped through. His officers collected more than one hundred tips about Cook's location, but none led anywhere. The chatter of tips only pulled searchers madly in all directions. They needed help, Laberge decided. At his request, seventy soldiers and Royal Canadian Air Force pilots joined the search.

Still, police spent the next two days getting nowhere. Searchers grew desperate. Officers even dynamited beaver dams to lower the water level of local rivers to see if Cook's drowned body might lie beneath. Perhaps he fell into a deep pool, police reasoned. Cook wasn't in any of them.

On the afternoon of July 14, pig farmer Norman Dufva spotted a strange man as he entered his long, wooden barn just south of Bashaw, fifty-two kilometres from the Ponoka Mental Institution. Dufva ran into his house, grabbed his shotgun, and yelled at his wife to call police. Her hands shook as she dialled.

Dufva kept his barn door closed and stood outside. He was content to keep Cook inside the barn rather than fight him. He might have a gun. He might run if Dufva let him know he'd been spotted.

Dufva needn't have bothered standing guard. Cook was spent.

Laberge arrived himself with three other officers. The four of them walked into the barn with apprehension that lasted only until they spotted Cook. They didn't even draw their guns.

"He was completely exhausted," Laberge would later recall.

Cook was slumped on the floor, dehydrated, hungry, and weak. There was a pile of clothes beside him. His face was dark with stubble and scarred from the car crash in the Monarch during his escape. Cook watched silently as the officers approached and made no move to flee. He was unarmed. There was a long silence in the barn.

Laberge was prepared. He offered a small package to Cook.

"Ham sandwich," the officer told him.

Cook tore into the sandwich and pointed at the clothes on the floor. "Those belong to the car I stole."

RCMP arrested Cook and took him to the nearest detachment in Bashaw. Half the town, two hundred people, crowded outside to catch a glimpse of the famous fugitive. Laberge then moved him to the more secure Fort Saskatchewan Jail, rather than back to Ponoka.

Reporters gathered around Laberge to hear how he finally caught Cook.

"You know," the officer said. "That boy was just a hop, a step, and a jump ahead of us all the way through. After he'd eaten and gained some strength, we asked him about different places he had visited and he said he'd been there ahead of us in almost all those places."

Five months later, on the last day of November 1959, Cook was led into the Red Deer courthouse handcuffed to a police officer.

Cook testified in his own defence for ten hours before a captivated courtroom. He denied committing any of the murders and claimed he was stunned to learn of them in his Stettler holding cell.

"It's hard to explain," he said in a low voice as he stared at his feet. "If you found out your family was all killed and you'd been charged with murder, it's hard to understand. The only thing I knew about the whole thing was that I didn't do it."

Prosecutors presented evidence that proved otherwise. A suit Cook had stitched for himself in prison was found in the family home covered in blood. Numerous items from the Cook house were found in the white convertible he was so proud of, including children's report cards and his father's marriage certificate. They were next to a suitcase filled with children's pyjamas and a photo album with pictures of his deceased mother.

Though prosecutors did not present a motive, Cook was convicted and a hanging date was set for April 15, 1960.

Three weeks before the noose, Cook's conviction was overturned by the Supreme Court of Alberta and he was granted a new trial. Cook's window of hope was open only a month, until June 1960, when the second trial reached the same conclusion as the first. Cook took the stand, denied the murders, and was convicted. It took the jury only twenty-two minutes of deliberation to decide.

Amid gasps of surprise in the court gallery, Cook remained as calm as ever as he was convicted for the second time, exactly one year after his crimes were discovered.

This time, there was no appeal.

Cook walked to the gallows with a level stride and maintained his innocence to the end.

He was hung at 12:05 a.m. on November 15, 1960.

"He went like a man," Warden Thomas Holt said of the last person ever hung by the province of Alberta.

EIGHTY-EIGHT BULLETS

Darnell Bass and Patrick Steven Ryan crouched in the shadows of the bank as they waited for the clock to strike midnight. The pair were hidden in the CIBC branch at Calgary's North Hill Shopping Centre in anticipation of a cash delivery from a Brink's armoured car. Bass, a thirty-one-year-old sergeant based at Canadian Forces Base Petawawa in Ontario, held an Austrian assault rifle. His friend since their teenage years, thirty-year-old Ryan, cradled an AK-47. The plan was supposed to be simple. They would surprise the guards who entered the bank and steal the bags of money they brought inside. Ryan had even written instructions for the guards on an easel and drawn a happy face next to them. Ryan didn't want to talk because they might recognize his voice from when he had worked at Brink's the previous year.

Earlier that evening of March 19, 1998, the pair made their final preparations in a hotel room a short drive away. They loaded ammunition clips with bullets and donned dark pants and sweaters with Brink's patches on the shoulders. They strapped on body armour and checked the tear gas canisters Bass had stolen from the Canadian Forces. Everything they needed was packed into silver cases like the ones carried by Brink's employees. Ryan donned a grey wig, glasses, and a moustache. He'd modelled them for his girlfriend days before, and she'd only recognized his eyes. Bass didn't bother with a disguise. Around 10:30, they pulled up to the dark mall in a rented van.

The pair used master keys they'd obtained to get inside the mall and then into the bank. The uniforms they wore duped cleaners into believing they were on the job.

Once alone, they waited.

The long-time friends deeply wanted to pull off a successful robbery. This was their fourth attempt after two years of planning. The first try at stealing from an ATM was foiled when keys they'd paid for didn't fit the locks. A New Year's Eve plan to hijack a truck was derailed when two trucks instead of one, along with twice as many guards, arrived at the ambush point. On New Year's Day, they'd waited in a van in a Calgary parking lot for hours for another armoured truck that never arrived.

The previous year, during a planning session, Bass asked what a Brink's guard would do with a gun in his face.

"To answer your question, they won't do a fucking thing," Ryan told him. "Look, I work for these guys. Security sucks. The guards are just there to keep the insurance companies happy. Trust me."

The lock on the front door of the CIBC bank turned.

It was early, Bass thought. 11:53. The guards weren't scheduled to arrive until after midnight.

Both men counted to five and stepped out with rifles raised and gas masks on their faces. The two Brink's guards, Brad Weber and Paul Bisson, stopped in surprise. Both dropped the grey bags of cash they carried.

Bisson, himself a former soldier, ignored the instructions on the easel, drew his revolver, and fired a wayward shot at Bass.

Ryan and Bass opened up with their assault rifles above the heads of the guards as they dove to the floor. For nearly three minutes, the pair fired a swarm of bullets that kept the guards pinned down. On the floor, Bisson and Weber were covered in shattered glass, shredded venetian blinds, and chunks of the wall. Bullets slammed into the Sailor's Steamer Hot Dogs next door and exploded the windows of a nearby Safeway. The gunmen chattered out eighty-eight shots between them.

The heist couldn't be salvaged, and Bass knew it. The bags of money were right there. He could see them, but he couldn't get close enough to pick them up without getting shot. They needed to get out.

"Gas! Gas!" Bass yelled.

Ryan took his finger off the trigger and tossed tear gas canisters to the floor. The friends fled through the acrid clouds that billowed through the bank without a penny of the $385,000 the guards had brought inside.

They sprinted to the rental van and ripped off their gas masks. They hurried back to their hotel.

"Did you hit anybody?" Bass asked.

"I don't know," Ryan said.

The pair shredded the fake uniforms and returned their rented van to Banff. On the way, they tossed what ammunition was left into random snowbanks. Bass waited two days in Canmore before his flight back to Ontario, and Ryan returned to Calgary.

The pair hadn't been caught when plans went wrong before, but none of their plans ever went this wrong. At least the two Brink's guards had escaped unharmed, the news reported.

In the 1980s, Bass and Ryan met as young cadets in the Royal Regina Rifles, a reserve infantry unit based in the Saskatchewan city. Bass was remembered as a gung-ho solider dedicated to military life, while Ryan was quieter and withdrawn. Ryan, the son of a doctor from an affluent family, left the regiment in 1985 to study French at the University of Regina but would later return to serve three more years. Bass, the son of an RCMP officer, remained in the military, moved to Ontario, and became a highly trained paratrooper in the ill-fated Canadian Airborne Regiment. The two men kept in contact. They spent holidays together and took long motorcycle trips across the country.

"I've known Darnell Bass for twenty years and I love him like a brother," Ryan would later tell the *Calgary Herald*.

Bass became the centre of national scandal in the early 1990s as part of the Canadian Airborne Regiment, after behaviour problems culminated in the beating death of a teenager during a mission in Somalia. The unit was disbanded in 1995. Bass, a seven-year paratrooper in the regiment, became angry and disillusioned with the military as a result.

"All my life I had followed all the rules and gave everything I had, and suddenly they change the rules on you," he later told the CBC. "Well, I thought it was my turn to take. I wanted to better myself and leave the military and I felt that getting a large sum of money would have helped set me up and start a new life."

A month after the robbery, Bass testified at a House of Commons committee and told them what the Airborne disbandment did to him: "It's like someone ripped my heart out and stomped on my guts."

During that testimony, four weeks after he shot up a bank, Bass told politicians honour had faded from the Canadian Forces. "We're here for Canada, we're here for Canadians, we're here to defend the country. But a lot of guys I'm hearing from these days, especially the young guys, are just in it for the money. The honour has gone away. You do not want an army with guys who are just in it for the money, because that sucks."

For weeks, Bass went about his military duties as usual while Calgary police hunted him. Robbery detectives paid particular attention to the tear gas canisters left at the scene. There were few places to obtain the gas, and police began to track them all. When forensic tests on the canisters concluded they were military, the trail led to the Canadian Forces, then to Bass.

Detectives arrested Bass at CFB Petawawa four months after the shootout at the North Hill Shopping Centre, on July 16. The same day, tactical officers raided several homes in the Ottawa area and emerged with an arsenal of weapons.

Investigators also knew all about Ryan, but couldn't find him. A Canada-wide arrest warrant was issued for him as tactical officers blew the door off his basement suite in Calgary a week after Bass was arrested. They seized weapons and Ryan's computer, but also found volumes of material on the Second World War, Hitler's Germany, and the Nazi regime.

Investigators suspected they wouldn't find Ryan in Canada. He hadn't been spotted in Calgary in several weeks, not since he had pawned two handguns at a southeast shop. He told the owner he needed quick money for a long trip.

As police raided Ryan's apartment, Bass made a court appearance in Calgary that seemed ripped from Hollywood. Officers had grown nervous when grenade launchers were found during a raid of the Ottawa-area homes of Bass's associates. Officers feared a possible escape or an attempt to kill Bass to keep him silent.

Tactical officers from the Calgary police met his plane on the runway and escorted him through the city, with more officers in a helicopter overhead. Snipers watched the five-block stretch between police headquarters and the courthouse, while officers cleared the courtroom and inspected every inch of it before Bass was brought inside. Anyone seated in the court gallery passed through a metal detector years before such security was commonplace at Alberta's courthouses. Six tactical officers accompanied Bass during his minute-long appearance.

After nearly two weeks in the wind, officers picked up Ryan's trail. They learned a Calgary repair shop, Anderwerks, had recently completed work on his prized BMW GS motorcycle. An order had been placed to equip the rough-road bike with a larger gas tank for longer trips. Once the work was complete, the bike was scheduled for transport to England. Ryan told the shop workers he'd been hired by a British journalist. She was about to start an assignment in South Africa and needed a guide, he said.

Dave Anderson, an Anderwerks employee, had worked on Ryan's bikes for years and never suspected he was a thief. After Anderson's last job, Ryan tipped him with a box of Bernard Callebaut chocolates.

Interpol officers captured Ryan on August 4 as he entered northwestern France at the port of Cherbourg. He'd arrived by ferry across the English Channel.

Ryan was treated better in custody at the French town of Caen than Bass was amid tight security in Canada. Ryan wrote a letter to the *Calgary Herald* from the writing desk in his large cell, next to a toilet and sink, two windows, and a television with eleven channels. There was a canteen where he could buy chocolate, cheese, Coke, and beer.

"It's quite bearable," Ryan wrote. He referred to himself as a celebrity who required isolation.

In November, with Ryan still in France, Bass admitted everything in a Calgary courtroom and pleaded guilty to conspiracy. He'd supplied the weaponry and stolen tear gas for the North Hill job. The equipment was his and the plan was Ryan's, Bass said. He was sentenced to seven years in prison.

It was February 1998 before Ryan moved through the extradition process and was put on a plane to Calgary.

The pair saw each other again at Ryan's trial. Ryan watched from the prisoner's box as Bass testified about the whole botched plan.

Ryan was sentenced to eight years in prison, one more than his long-time friend.

THE PRETENDER

Mark Andrew Twitchell strode through crowds at Edmonton's Shaw Conference Centre with great pride in his enormous, bright yellow robot costume. People stepped out of his way to avoid its six-foot wingspan. He relished the stares from fellow costumed revellers at the 2007 Halloween Howler party sponsored by a local radio station. Many in attendance recognized him immediately as a science-fiction character named Bumblebee from the *Transformers* films. The attention was his reward for weeks of solitary, painstaking work in his St. Albert basement, boiling, molding, and painting plastic. He considered himself a master craftsman, obsessed with every detail.

"For two months I slaved on this thing, pushing past test fittings, setbacks, redos and adjustments until finally he was ready for the world," Twitchell wrote.

That night, he won first prize in the party's costume contest and left with $3,000 and a Harley-Davison motorcycle. Of all Twitchell's costumes, Bumblebee was the most successful.

More than anything, Twitchell liked to play make-believe. The thirty-one-year-old fan stole costume ideas from movies and stories he admired. He dressed as human and alien characters from the *Star Wars* films. He disguised himself as Wolverine, Iron Man, and other characters lifted from comic books. All of his costumes were homemade with meticulous care. Twitchell showed up in costume where he'd be most appreciated, at movie premieres or *Star Wars* conventions. He made sure to pose for pictures each time and posted them enthusiastically on Facebook.

"I find few things in life as exhilarating and a total blast as partying on Halloween with a crazy kick-ass costume, preferably of my own design," he wrote.

Twitchell, a baby-faced man with short dark hair, was an aspiring film director. He made his own unauthorized *Star Wars* movie after scraping together $35,000 from investors and assembling an experienced crew. He completed the film, but almost no one other than Twitchell's friends and family ever saw it.

In 2008, he wrote and filmed *House of Cards*, a short film about a serial killer who targeted sinners. He borrowed liberally from the American television series *Dexter*, which had a similar premise. Later that year, he wrote a scene about an Edmonton man murdered in a garage. Twitchell had already rented one to use as a setting.

He wrote about the murder from a personal perspective on his home computer.

"This story is based on true events," Twitchell wrote in his diary. "This is the story of my progression into becoming a serial killer."

When the police came for him, Twitchell insisted the diary was a fictional script, just more make-believe. He was only pretending.

***

Johnny Altinger's disappearance was suspicious in every possible way.

The quiet, reserved man spent much of his time on the internet in his tidy bachelor's home. Johnny had a lifelong interest in computers and aptitude for technology. Most of his friends met him online before they met in person. Besides his computer, a pair of motorcycles were his most prized possessions. He kept the bikes in pristine condition, and even arranged for friends to keep them covered while he was away.

By late 2008, thirty-eight-year-old Johnny had dedicated himself to finding a wife. He was comfortable shuffling through the profiles of local singles on dating websites in search of his perfect match. In October, he thought he might have found her. Her name was Jen, and her profile picture showed a beautiful brunette posing in a bikini on a beach. She seemed almost too good to be true, and she agreed to meet him on a Saturday night.

When Johnny told his friend about the date, Dale Smith wanted to be happy for him, but inside he had doubts. Jen told Johnny via email that she wanted to meet in an alley garage in a south Edmonton neighbourhood. Smith thought it was weird.

Give me a call when you get there, he told Johnny.

To ease his friend's nerves, Johnny emailed him directions to the garage.

No one heard from Johnny after the date until two days later, when friends and family received a bizarre email. He was with the mysterious Jen on a long tropical vacation to her summer home in Costa Rica, the note said. The date was so fantastic, she took him to Central America.

"I've got a one-way ticket to heaven and I'm not coming back," a second message read. His Facebook status changed from 'Single' to 'In a Relationship.' His boss received an email that said the dependable Johnny was quitting his job.

Friends didn't think the surprise emails sounded like Johnny. They lacked his usual pleasantries and nicknames. No one believed he would dash away on an impulsive trip. His motorcycles weren't covered when Smith and other friends visited his home a week later. Johnny would never leave the country with his bikes like that. Inside the house, friends found his passport, shaving kit, and empty luggage. They called the police.

The Costa Rica story was bull. Anyone who knew Johnny could see that, and it didn't take long for police to reach the same conclusion.

There was no Jen. Someone had staged the whole thing.

* * *

At first, police considered Altinger a missing person. Murder investigations weren't opened solely on the word of suspicious friends. In a city the size of Edmonton, people left their usual lives for a few days all the time.

Just in case, a team of officers called a list of contacts from Altinger's computer. Two homicide detectives also took part, but Bill Clark and Mark Anstey didn't believe the case was a murder. Altinger was likely safe at some girl's place in Edmonton, they thought. Nothing in his condo suggested any trouble. No forced entry, no blood.

The police met Mark Twitchell early in the investigation only because Altinger had given Dale Smith the address to the rented garage. Twitchell told police he didn't know Jen and had never heard of Johnny Altinger. The would-be director seemed forthcoming and helpful as he answered every question police put to him. He gave them permission to go into the garage if they came to St. Albert to pick up the keys. He was on his way to visit his parents, Twitchell explained.

That night, Detective Brian Murphy met him in a convenience store parking lot. Twitchell told the officer a strange story as they chatted in the front seat of Murphy's car. Earlier in October, he said, a man knocked on his car window at a gas station and asked if he wanted to buy a car. The man had met a wealthy woman who wanted to take him on a trip. He didn't need the vehicle any more, and Twitchell could have it for whatever money was in his wallet. He bought the car for forty bucks, and it was parked at a friend's house.

Murphy knew he should call in Twitchell's ridiculous tale. The story stunk. As Twitchell sat in the passenger seat, Murphy called Anstey in the homicide unit. Anstey listened, then covered the phone and told Clark about the red Mazda Twitchell miraculously bought for forty bucks. It was the same make and colour as Johnny Altinger's car.

"Holy Fuck!" Clark exclaimed. "He killed the guy!"

Clark kept Twitchell at police headquarters all night. He used one of the "softer" interview rooms, with a couch.

Twitchell was talkative and even wrote out an eight-page statement. Just before 5:00 a.m., the detective bluntly told the wannabe filmmaker investigators knew he was involved in Altinger's disappearance. After hours of interrogation, Twitchell hadn't implicated himself enough to arrest him. The detective needed more proof, and the police had to let him go.

As he was leaving, Clark turned to Twitchell with a smile and pointed to a Pontiac Grand Am in the parking lot of downtown headquarters. "Is that your car right there?"

"Yeah."

"I'm seizing your car."

* * *

The evidence against Twitchell mounted, and he was put under police surveillance. Police found the *House of Cards* script about a man who met a mystery woman at a garage and ended up murdered. There were bloodstains in the Mazda's trunk and in Twitchell's Pontiac. Knives and a pipe found in the rented garage had more blood on them. Forensics found Altinger's DNA on Twitchell's clothes.

Technical investigators discovered Twitchell's incriminating diary on his home computer. Homicide detectives had never seen evidence like this before. Days' worth of details in the supposedly fictional killer's life, everything from where he ate to where he ran errands. More than a hundred police officers were involved in the Twitchell investigation, and several of them tried to prove as much of the forty-page document as possible. They visited the restaurants from the story and showed his picture to waitresses. Most of the story's contents mirrored Twitchell's real life perfectly.

Investigators were shocked to discover Twitchell had written about a previous victim who had escaped alive. Police later concluded that a week before Altinger's mystery date, an Edmonton man named Gilles Tetreault visited Twitchell's garage to meet a woman. That time, it was a blonde named Sheena who had agreed to a date on the same website Altinger used. They were supposed to meet at the garage, then have dinner and see a movie.

When he arrived, Tetreault was attacked by a man in a painted hockey mask wielding a stun gun. The two men struggled until the masked man pulled a gun and wrapped duct tape over Tetreault's eyes.

Blind and terrified on the cement floor, Tetreault thought he was about to die.

"I decided I better fight back, because I thought I'd rather die my way than his way," he said of the ordeal.

Again, the two men fought, and Tetreault realized the gun was fake. He escaped the garage and never reported the bizarre attack until he saw a report of Altinger's murder on the news.

Despite the progress in the case, police still didn't have Altinger's body. Aside from the blood, there was no sign of him, and Twitchell wasn't talking. He refused to confess after months in his isolated cell at the Edmonton Remand Centre. His diary mentioned dumping a body into the sewer, but that left thousands of possibilities across Edmonton. Detectives offered a court-ordered release for a day if he led police to the body. Twitchell said no.

Finally, in June 2010, Twitchell sent a message to the homicide unit through his lawyer. Twitchell wanted to meet, and would give them something as long as they didn't ask questions or talk to the press. Also, Detective Clark wasn't invited. The police agreed.

In an interview room, Twitchell slid a piece of paper across the table to Detective Brad Mandrusiak, then left without a word. It was a map, printed from the internet, with directions to a manhole cover in a north Edmonton alley, blocks from where Twitchell's parents lived.

That night, in the dark and narrow alley, Mandrusiak shined a flashlight down a sewer grate and found what remained of Johnny Altinger.

In the spring of 2011, Twitchell's trial attracted news coverage and curiosity from across North America. Prosecutors proved he lured Altinger inside the detached garage he rented for his film. When Altinger arrived for his "date," Twitchell bashed his head in with a copper pipe and stabbed him. He dismembered his victim and dropped the body parts through a manhole.

It was all a mistake, Twitchell testified, just a cinematic hoax he'd created that went wrong. He'd posed as Jen on the dating website, he admitted to the jury, and Altinger was furious to discover the ruse. Twitchell claimed Altinger attacked him with a pipe, and he stabbed him in self-defence. He admitted to dismembering his victim and disposing of his body. He used Altinger's key to enter his home and send the messages about Costa Rica.

The hoax on Altinger was intended as part of a campaign for his movie project, he explained. The trick was the same one the killer used in his *House of Cards* script. Twitchell was proud of his cinematic genius, as he called it.

"It's something like a subconscious, innate savant power," he told a full courtroom.

It took five hours for the jury to find him guilty. They decided Twitchell was still pretending.

CANNIBAL

Swift Runner appeared curiously healthy for a man who had just barely survived a brutal winter alongside a large family that had starved to death. During the spring thaw of 1879, the Cree guide walked back into civilization with a horrible story of his last few tragic months, but appeared fit and strong. Residents of the Roman Catholic mission in St. Albert noted the tall man hadn't lost much off his thick, two-hundred pound frame. It seemed unbelievable someone so big had only eaten boiled strips of his teepee to survive, as he claimed.

Swift Runner reached the mission in March, as winter faded. In the fall, he'd entered the woods of Sturgeon County with his mother, brother, wife, and six children. Months later, he came out alone.

Previously, he'd been a guide for the Hudson's Bay Company along trapping lines in the territories that would eventually become part of northern Alberta. In 1875, when members of the North-West Mounted Police reached the area, Swift Runner was recommended to officers as an experienced, knowledgeable guide. He spoke enough English to be popular with white men who feared losing their way in the forests.

Still, spending time with Swift Runner was not for the faint of heart. As a NWMP officer later wrote, the guide has as "ugly and evil-looking a face as I have ever seen."

Alcohol was banned in the territory at the time, but dark bottles of whiskey disguised as patent medicine were still easy to find. The Cree guide found a lot of them.

"Swift Runner became inordinately fond of it and when half-drunk was the terror of the whole region," read a *Manitoba Free Press* article. "Six feet and three in height, and of extraordinary strength, he was an ugly customer to meet when on a spree, and the police gave him a wide berth on such occasions."

At the St. Albert mission, the priests were eager to hear Swift Runner's story of his family's fate. Winter conditions had never been more desperate, the guide explained. There were no animals to trap or shoot. Supplies the family carried to sustain them until hunts improved dwindled quickly.

Weeks into the cold, exhausted and hungry, the family resorted to trapping rodents and squirrels. Still, those meagre meals were not enough to keep them alive. Eventually, the family cut strips of rawhide from their tents, boiled them, and choked down what they could. His youngest died first, Swift Runner told them. The other children followed. His mother and brother left camp determined to find food and never returned. His wife, despondent over the deaths of her children, killed herself. He said he'd buried them all.

Swift Runner's story was suspicious for reasons other than his weight. The priests at the St. Albert mission heard from other Aboriginals that the winter hunt was plentiful. This didn't necessarily mean Swift Runner was lying, though he often screamed in his sleep and complained of nightmares. The priests allowed him to live among them until he asked if the mission's children could accompany him on a hunting trip. Their trust stretched to its limit, the priests asked officers to verify Swift Runner's story.

Local NWMP officers were less willing to trust the gruesome tale when Swift Runner walked into their post in Fort Saskatchewan. They'd heard rumours. A Cree chief cryptically told them Swift Runner ate well that winter. A fellow hunter swore the family was murdered in the woods, not starved. In the last weeks of winter, before Swift Runner returned, a number of officers tried, and failed, to find his family. No one knew if the rumours were true.

Inspector Severe Gagnon didn't believe the starvation story. The officer with the high forehead and beard hanging down to his chest was once a lawyer in Montreal. He had experience separating fact from fiction.

Take us to your camp, Gagnon ordered Swift Runner. Show us your family's graves.

In the spring, Swift Runner led officers back to the scene of his tragic tale. They searched for days. Twice he tried to escape but was hauled back to camp. He walked around in circles until Gagnon finally realized there were no graves to find. Swift Runner hadn't buried anyone.

Near the charred remains of a campfire, officers found clumps of dark hair among the dry bones of Swift Runner's family. A child's moccasin was stuffed inside his mother's skull. They found more bones emptied of marrow. The tents the family had supposedly eaten were tangled up in the trees nearby. Officers also found a kettle with thick, fatty sludge inside. The camp lacked any sign of animal tracks, disproving Swift Runner's claim that scavenging predators dug up the bodies.

Swift Runner returned to Fort Saskatchewan a prisoner.

His trial was held in August. A jury of six, four of whom spoke Cree, convicted him of murder and cannibalism after twenty minutes of deliberation.

"I am going to tell the whole truth," Swift Runner finally confessed. "I have done a great deal of wrong, and that was the reason I was backward at telling about it. I did not kill anybody's children but my own."

He shot two of his sons near the camp before he shot his wife in the chest. Swift Runner caved in the skulls of his older daughters with an axe, then strangled his youngest daughter. After a long walk with his remaining son, the father shot him in the head near the shore of Big Lake.

Swift Runner claimed he knew nothing of his mother and brother's deaths.

"My wife said nothing to me when I killed our second boy. I never before threatened to kill and eat my wife. I have told you everything I know I have done."

Swift Runner's hanging took place before sunrise on a frigid December morning. Sixty people gathered in Fort Saskatchewan to watch the first hanging in the territory.

An hour before he was supposed to drop, the crowd stole the wooden trap from the gallows and burned it for warmth as they waited.

As the trap was replaced, Swift Runner sat near an open fire and ate a last meal of pemmican, the noose already roped around his neck.

"I could kill myself with a tomahawk," he said, "and save the hangman further trouble."

The St. Albert mission offered Swift Runner a priest, but the Cree shook his head. The white man ruined me, he said, so their God could not be worth much.

Gagnon walked him to the gallows. The officer's breath plumed around his beard and thick buffalo coat. Swift Runner thanked Gagnon for treating him well, then made fun of him for moving so slowly in the brutal cold.

The hangman pulled a black hood over Swift Runner's head and led him onto the trap. He fell five feet, died quickly, and was buried in the snow outside Fort Saskatchewan.

NICK'S MILLIONS

Nicholas Edward Lysyk lived two lives.

Each morning, he arrived at the Bank of Montreal branch in a west Edmonton strip mall where he worked precisely half an hour before any of his co-workers. He was a pudgy man with glasses, and wore a toupée to cover his faded hairline. Most days, he would get a chocolate bar or ice cream at the Husky gas station across the street. At the same time each day, to the minute, he would drive home.

"Your typical nerd banker," one neighbour said. "You have that picture in your head of what a banker should look like and he is totally that. He is a very, very straight guy."

Lysyk possessed no presence, people said. He was a man no one noticed unless he slouched directly into their field of vision.

He wore golf shirts, dark suits, and loafers. He rarely drank and told people he'd quit smoking because it was bad for his wallet, not his health. He shared a clean house and a manicured lawn with his wife, Jennifer. Lysyk had no criminal record and was never in trouble.

"Frankly, they were pretty boring," their neighbours said.

At times, co-workers and friends noticed Lysyk drove a luxury car, though no one gave it much thought. He wasn't the first middle-aged banker to buy an expensive car.

Nick and Jennifer were high school sweethearts from Mundare, a town east of Edmonton best known for a forty-two-foot statue of its famous sausage next to the highway. Lysyk, the second child of five, had just graduated from high school and was working on a business administration degree when he met the fifteen-year-old Jennifer. They were married three years later, in 1972.

Eventually, the dull version of Lysyk's life went into the red. He and Jennifer suffered financially in the early 1990s and nearly lost their house to foreclosure when they missed mortgage payments. In 1993, Lysyk filed for bankruptcy. At the time, the couple owned a decade-old Oldsmobile worth $5,000 and a Chevette worth $2,000. Their relationship suffered, and they spent less time together.

Lysyk's second life began in 1996, in his early fifties, and was far more interesting.

It was a fantasyland where the banker had fourteen girlfriends spread across the Edmonton area, all of them connected to massage parlours and escort services he visited regularly. He would buy drinks for random young women at bars in the West Edmonton Mall and tell them a sad, lonely story about how his wife had left him.

The women had never met anyone like Lysyk. Money poured out of him, along with vehicles, homes, jewelry, and anything else with a large price tag. He gave them credit cards in his name and told them to pose as his wife. Friends and family also benefited with new wheels in the driveways of well-stocked homes.

Lysyk lived a high life for a man who never made more than $61,000 a year. He told everyone he'd received a huge amount of money in his aunt's will.

Nick and Jennifer legally separated in September 2001. He moved out, but they never signed divorce papers.

Lysyk was promoted to manager of the Wolf Willow neighbourhood branch of the Bank of Montreal in April 2002.

Four months later, he arrived at work early as always. Another bank employee was scrutinizing a stack of standard audits when a loan for $290,000 caught her eye. It was issued only days earlier in the name of Lillian Green.

The paperwork seemed in order, but Green's handwriting looked similar to that of the bank employee who authorized it, Nick Lysyk.

He was fired within hours. For once, Lysyk left work early.

The Bank of Montreal investigated and found the first traces of one of the largest bank frauds Canada had ever seen.

Six days later, he was arrested and his life exploded.

The massive fraud leapt onto the front pages of newspapers and topped every newscast. Tawdry, lavish details of his life entertained Edmontonians for months.

The search began for the missing millions Lysyk had stolen though fraudulent loans. Teams of investigators and receivers collected piles of court orders and repossessed homes, cars, and furniture. The assets of a downtown massage parlour were seized until officers could determine how they were paid for. The bank wanted everything Lysyk had bought with its money over six years. They just needed to find it all.

A criminal charge and a Bank of Montreal lawsuit landed in courtrooms within two weeks of each other. Lysyk was charged with fraud over $5,000, but that description didn't do his crimes justice.

The quiet banker had created sixty-four fraudulent loans worth more than $16 million. The lies began in December 1996, a year after his promotion to financial services manager, and never stopped. He hadn't even started small. The first fraudulent loan was for $75,000.

Lysyk knew the loan system well. He knew how people got caught. He used demand loans that only required interest payments to remain in good standing. The small amount of interest he did pay was financed through further illegal loans in the names of existing customers or people he invented from thin air. All the proceeds were funnelled into six bank accounts in his own name.

The scheme made a profit of just over $14 million after Lysyk paid off the interest.

It took two years of investigation and court hearings to find out where it all went.

Lysyk kept $4 million for himself and gave most of what remained to women. His wife received a million in cash and property. Lillian Green, whom Lysyk met at a massage parlour, received more than $3 million. His family and long-time friends collected $1.5 million in gifts. At least twenty-three people—all "wilfully blind," the bank said—got richer. All of them hired lawyers in the weeks after the frumpy bank manager was arrested.

Lysyk's shopping list was long. The stolen millions were used to buy seventeen houses and condominiums, a cottage at Sandy Lake, a houseboat, a set of lawn equipment, furniture, expensive clothes, and hundreds of other items. Credit cards he gave to women he barely knew racked up charges for nearly $4 million worth of merchandise.

The city's jewelry stores made a killing off Lysyk. He once bought an $18,000 diamond ring for Green and a $6,000 watch for his daughter. He dropped ten grand on a pair of earrings. Lysyk bought from one saleswoman at each store he visited, and they all recognized their best customer on the news. One clerk was named a top seller in her national chain solely because of him. All the clerks heard his well-practiced sob story about a failed marriage and an inheritance from his aunt that he'd invested.

"If a banker can't make money from his investments, who can?" one clerk later asked investigators.

Lysyk purchased forty vehicles during his six-year fraud spree. Gone was his old Chevette from 1993. His fleet now included a Mercedes Benz, a BMW, a Jeep, and several muscle cars reminiscent of his youth, including a 1971 Dodge Demon. The crown jewel was a black-and-yellow replica 1971 Plymouth Hemi Barracuda. Lysyk spent $100,000 on the collector's dream. On weekends, he would drive the 425-horsepower engine to a St. Albert parking lot to show off to fellow car buffs. His licence plate read MY CUDA.

Millions were still unaccounted for even after all the lavish goods were seized. Investigators didn't believe it was hidden, just gone.

Lysyk told police he was a victim himself. Some of his various women eventually left and blackmailed him for more money on the way out. Those women and their real boyfriends extorted him out of a million in cash, he said.

Greg Marshall, the husband of a female friend of Lysyk's, received more than $125,000. In police interviews, he denied any threats or extortion. Still, the banker had been used.

He was a "sugar daddy and a mark," Marshall told investigators.

The crook spent six fearful weeks in the Edmonton Remand Centre before he was released on bail. Behind bars, he was both famous and vulnerable among the hundreds of other men who awaited trial.

As the Bank of Montreal demanded money from Jennifer, she withdrew $200,000 from one of her bank accounts and gave it to Brian Beresh, a top defence lawyer in Edmonton. It was for bail, she said, and to defend her husband against the criminal charges. Family and friends chipped in to spring Lysyk on $500,000 bail.

The Lysyks reconciled while he lived on a childhood friend's acreage near Mundare as part of his strict bail conditions. Jennifer visited him on weekends and Wednesday evenings.

During his lawsuit battle, he filed documents that blamed the Bank of Montreal for "employing policies and practices that were inadequate to monitor and control its operations, including the approval and documentation of loans."

Lysyk stood and told his civil trial, "It is the big, bad bank against me."

With his account frozen and legal bills to pay, Lysyk quickly became poor. He told court he applied for work at fifty-nine companies and none returned his calls. He eventually applied for welfare and asked the legal-aid office to fund his defence. He was denied. The bank demanded he pay rent on the condo he later moved into with Jennifer because it was an asset frozen by the bank.

"That's just mean-spirited, in my opinion," Beresh told reporters.

Lysyk complained the Bank of Montreal never paid his severance and withheld holiday pay they owed him. Eventually, the former millionaire was forced to visit food banks and filed for bankruptcy for the second time in his life.

By June 2004, Nick and Jennifer were separated again.

A month later, a receivership auction sold much of what remained of Lysyk's fantasy life. It was the largest auction of its kind in Edmonton, topping the one for Peter Pocklington, the reviled former owner of the Edmonton Oilers.

The Hemi Barracuda sold for $110,000.

In August 2004, Lysyk, now a slouched and tired fifty-four-year-old, pleaded guilty to one count of fraud that covered all his criminal loans.

His version of the story emerged in court through a forensic psychologist who interviewed the former banker. Lysyk claimed he committed his crimes due to depression over his wife's affair and later the blackmail he'd claimed to police.

"Whenever I tried to pull back I was threatened," he told Dr. Marc Nesca. "I always gave money thinking it would be the last time."

Jennifer, then the only women Lysyk had ever dated, cheated on him in 1997, and he'd been depressed ever since, Nesca said.

Lysyk claimed his family pressured him for gifts and that his daughter test drove a Jaguar into his bank's parking lot and told him to buy it. It was only pressure from other people that forced him to create the fake loans, he said.

Crown prosecutor Sheila Brown had another theory.

"Greed," she told the packed courtroom.

A month later, Lysyk was sentenced to seven years and four months in jail. In court, he buried his face in his hands and said nothing.

He scribbled a note and gave it to Beresh to read to reporters outside the courthouse.

"I apologize to everyone that I have hurt through my conduct. I want the public to know that Jennifer Lysyk knew nothing of my crime, nor did any of my family."

Lysyk was paroled fourteen months later.

In 2008, the Bank of Montreal gave up on its efforts to find all the stolen money. They recovered less than a third of the stolen $14 million.

PRISONERS OF WAR

Not all German prisoners were on the same side in Medicine Hat Internment Camp 132. The prisoner-of-war camp, one of five in Alberta, was crowded when it first opened and housed six thousand captive Germans. By 1943, the camp on the outskirts of town had doubled in population and swelled to 320 acres of tents, shacks, barbed wire, and guard towers. It was crowded. It was tense.

Older men from the Veterans Guard of Canada watched the perimeter. Inside the camp, the Germans were largely free to live as they pleased, provided no one tried to escape. The hundreds of guards, some old enough to have served in the First World War, were only there to keep the prisoners contained. Below the towers, the Nazis made their own meals, played their own sports, and lived their own limited lives. They formed their own hierarchies and alliances.

The camp supplied soccer balls and boxing gloves for the prisoners. At times, they were brought outside camp to grow their own produce or into Medicine Hat to help with supply deliveries. Outside the wire, prisoners wore dark blue overalls with a red bull's eye painted on the back.

The captives were from two strains of the German Army, those that once served in the French Foreign Legion and those who were always Nazi soldiers. In the 1930s, many members of Camp 132 had been Legion mercenaries and had fought in North Africa. Once they returned home to Germany, they were forced into re-education camps and enlisted in Nazi forces. Legionnaires were sent back to North Africa in the Second World War with swastikas on their uniforms because they knew the terrain. When the Allied forces prevailed in that part of the world, many Nazi soldiers blamed the Legionnaires among them. Almost all the Germans in the Medicine Hat camp were captured in North Africa.

The small number of Legionnaires were considered weak soldiers with weaker loyalty by the Nazi and Gestapo officers who held the camp's political power. The Legionnaires fed the suspicion of their fellow Germans when they only socialized with each other. Rumours of plots to overthrow the leadership of the camp spread quickly among the bored, captured soldiers.

August Plaszek and Christian Schultz were among the Legionnaires. Plaszek was a short, quiet man with no interest in camp politics. He and Schultz were thought to be part of the camp's underground.

A small mob grabbed the pair on the evening of July 22, 1943. The Nazi leaders of the camp set up a makeshift court in the recreation hall. It was just for a few innocent questions, the Legionnaires were told.

Schultz recognized the danger first. He bolted from the hall and past the growing mob outside. Schultz sprinted to the barbed-wire perimeter and approached the barbed wire forty-five feet inside the camp. As the guards shouted at him to stop, the terrified prisoner pulled a white handkerchief from his pocket and waved it madly as the Nazis chased him down. He barely reached safety in time.

Frustrated, the mob turned on Plaszek. He was bloodied by a rock to the head and dragged back into the recreational hall. Any pretence of a courtroom was tossed aside as Plaszek was beaten and interrogated about his supposed political plans. Eventually, he was dragged to a raised platform the captives used as a boxing ring and hung from a wooden support beam.

The next day, Schultz was transferred to another internment camp as the first murder investigation at Camp 132 began.

The Nazi officers continued to suspect the Legionnaires. Rumours spread and resentments festered as the camp grew by thousands. A twenty-eight-year-old Nazi, Sergeant Walter Wolf, kept a list of those Legionnaires chiefly suspected of treason.

Months passed and the Germans grew dour as it became apparent they might lose the war. By the summer of 1944, news of the assassination attempt on Adolf Hitler by his own officers reached Canada. Shortly after, the Nazi leader loudly proclaimed that German soldiers around the world should purge possible traitors among them. The news riled the captives as they huddled around radios to hear the latest reports. They read copies of the *Lethbridge Daily News* and the *Calgary Herald*, two newspapers dominated by war updates. There were enough English-speaking Germans around the camp to translate the headlines, including Karl Lehmann.

A professor of languages in his previous life, Lehmann was an unpopular teacher in his current one. He taught French to soldiers in one of the camp's classrooms. He spoke often of the possibility of Germany's defeat and was an open critic of Hitler. Some thought he showed a lack of sympathy for Germany when he read the newspapers aloud. Fellow captives heard he'd distributed Communist propaganda in a British internment camp years before. Even worse, to his fellow Nazis, he was friends with the Legionnaires.

Sergeant Major Bruno Perzonowsky was particularly disdainful of Lehmann. Perzonowsky's war had once gone well. The Luftwaffe pilot completed sixty missions and was twice honoured with the Iron Cross. Then he was shot down over Britain and had spent the past three years as a bitter prisoner of war. Perzonowsky told other Nazis they should eliminate traitors among them and become heroes once they returned home.

In early September 1944, Perzonowsky ordered the arrests of eighteen of the Legionnaires on Wolf's list for questioning about their conspiracy. Perzonowsky advocated for them all to hang, but they were eventually released back into the camp's tense population.

On September 10, Perzonowsky and other Nazi soldiers learned they were about to be transferred to an internment camp in Ontario. The official reason was to make room in Medicine Hat for prisoners taken in the Normandy landing, but the Nazis suspected they were being separated from the Legionnaires they hated.

Perzonowsky called a small meeting. He told Wolf it was his national duty to help kill Lehmann. Perzonowsky also recruited Sergeant Major Willi Mueller, the camp's boxing champion, and Sergeant Major Heinrich Busch, a burly pilot shot down over Britain. They could be court-martialled and shot once they returned to Germany if they refused to kill Lehmann, Perzonowsky told them.

The four lured Lehmann to his classroom, supposedly to sign certificates of language proficiency for captives headed to Ontario.

"Do you know anything about the Communist activities in this camp?" Perzonowsky asked.

They gave Lehmann no chance to answer. Mueller punched him in the face and Perzonowsky shoved a rag into his mouth.

The men wrapped a rope around Lehmann's neck, tied the other end to a gas pipe, and strangled him as he knelt on the floor. Guards found him the next morning.

RCMP Corporal Arthur Bull led the investigations into the murders of both Plaszek and Lehmann. Neither was solved quickly. German soldiers captive in enemy territory were loathe to turn on each other in the name of Canadian justice.

Eventually, it was Wolf who broke.

"I've decided to burn my bridges behind me," the soldier told Bull. "What I am about to tell is after I have given the matter consideration, and after I have had a great inward struggle."

In 1946, after the war ended, seven Germans were arrested in the two cases. They were transferred to the Lethbridge

Provincial Jail and held in cells isolated from a population that would welcome Germans coldly. Guards were constantly outside their cells and switched shifts every four hours.

Only one of three men on trial for Plaszek's murder was sentenced to die. Lieutenant Corporal Johannes Wittinger was acquitted, Private Adolf Krantz received a life sentence, and Sergeant Werner Schwalb, a tank gunner and Iron Cross recipient, was hung in June 1946.

He spoke five German words before the hangman pulled the hood over his head.

"My Fuehrer, I follow thee."

The following month, trials were under way for Lehmann's killers at the same time as Nazi leaders were charged and tried in Nuremberg. The guilty pleas came in rapid succession. One trial would conclude on Tuesday evening and another would begin Wednesday morning.

Prosecutors came to court with a twenty-three-page confession Wolf wrote about Lehmann's murder in the classroom. He'd even drawn a sketch that pinpointed where each German stood.

Mueller was asked if he had anything to say to the court, spectators, and assembled press.

"Nein," he said quietly.

Only Wolf gave the court any credit. "I stand here as a soldier of a foreign power which, until recently, was at war with Canada. I could not place full confidence in this court, but, through sitting in and listening to everything, it was shown to me and has fully convinced me that this trial was very fair."

Lawyer George Rice, of Lethbridge, appealed all four convictions. He argued the trials should've been held in a military court to ensure jurisdiction over prisoners of war. Rice also attempted to convince the court it had lost jurisdiction when Germany surrendered the previous year. The soldiers were still on active duty and couldn't be prosecuted for a murder committed under orders, the lawyer argued.

"I'm willing to grasp at every straw, my lord," Rice said in court.

The appeals were dismissed in October 1945. The defendants would hang in December.

For the next two months, the Germans remained separated from the rest of the Lethbridge prisoners. They played games of chess on separate boards in their cells and yelled moves down the concrete hallway.

The Germans were offended when an Alberta man joined their cellblock and was scheduled to hang beside them. Donald Sherman Staley had killed a seven-year-old boy during a sexual assault in July 1946.

Perzonowsky was furious that he would be hung next to a pedophile. The four Germans requested to die by firing squad, "as soldiers should," but were told all condemned men in Alberta died by the rope.

Still, the Germans refused to speak to Staley and excluded him from their chess games. The child killer did jigsaw puzzles instead.

On December 18, the day they were to hang, Mueller, Busch, and Perzonowsky slit their wrists with razor blades smuggled into their cells inside books. They preferred to die bleeding rather than swinging. Though the men were weakened by blood loss, guards reached them in time to bandage their arms and save them just hours before their execution.

A guard stopped at the fourth German cell and saw no blood.

"I didn't want to die that way," said Wolf, unhurt.

The Germans walked the gallows stairs in canvas slippers and were hung two at a time. Staley swung last. All ignored their chance to speak a few last words.

The five death sentences were the largest mass hanging in Alberta's history. The men were buried in separate coffins in the same grave.

MAYERTHORPE

A barrage of gunshots echoed from the long steel shed on the snowy farm outside Mayerthorpe. For a moment, Constable Garrett Hoogestraat thought his four fellow Mounties inside were pounding on the wall. Then more gunshots rang out, followed by screams. Outside the building, Hoogestraat and his partner, Corporal Stephen Vigor, were filled with dread. Both yanked their guns from their holsters.

The two officers had arrived at James Roszko's farm that morning of March 3, 2005, to seize stolen vehicle parts discovered in the farm's steel Quonset the day before. Four officers were already on site. Constables Anthony Gordon and Leo Johnston were posted overnight to guard the stolen parts and marijuana plants inside. Gordon was on loan from the Whitecourt detachment further west along Highway 43. His pregnant wife was awake and waiting for him to come home. Johnston, a motorcycle racer and expert marksman, had been a Mountie for four years. He and his twin brother, Lee, became officers around the same time.

Constable Peter Schiemann was in plain clothes because he planned to shop for detachment supplies in Edmonton. He'd given Constable Brock Myrol, a rookie officer on the job for less than three weeks, a ride to the farm to relieve the overnight shift. Other officers were on their way so Johnston and Gordon could go home and sleep. Aside from Schiemann, they all wore light body armour.

Hoogestraat and Vigor, both auto-theft investigators, chatted with the four younger officers as they readied their equipment and slid into overalls. It was a peaceful morning. The gun-loving Roszko had fled his property the previous day and was last seen driving across the country roads he'd terrorized for years as a bully and thug. He would turn up eventually, but would likely be another officer's problem. On the farm, all that was left to do was catalogue the stolen parts and count the marijuana plants in the back of the shed. Even Roszko's guard dogs were quiet after the officers fed them tranquilized meat.

Moments after the four officers walked from the bright sunshine into the dark Quonset, the gunfire began.

Hoogestraat and Vigor scrambled through the snow and mud to the front of the Quonset. The shots came in quick succession, likely from an automatic rifle. The two officers took cover behind police cruisers parked near the wide, open door. They paused. No more screams; no more shots. Hoogestraat risked a peek at the doorway. He could see a pair of legs inside, clothed in the navy blue and yellow stripe of a Mountie uniform. Beyond, the windowless Quonset was black inside.

"Call it in!" Vigor yelled. The officer was a part-time member of the heavily armed Emergency Response Team, and he'd been in bad situations before. The previous year, he had seen a fellow officer get shot during a standoff in Spruce Grove.

Hoogestraat called 911 on his cellphone. "We've got shots fired and we've got a member down! Numerous shots fired! Numerous shots fired!"

After the ambush, Roszko ventured outside and strolled across the farm police thought they could seize from him. The short, angry forty-six-year-old was heavy with guns. There was a pistol tucked under his belt, a Winchester rifle over his shoulder, and a semi-automatic rifle in his grip. He had pulled thick wool socks over his boots to silence his steps.

Vigor stared as Roszko walked into view. A brief twitch of surprise crossed the gunman's hard features before he fired twice. The car window near Vigor shattered in a spray of glass, and the side mirror exploded into fragments. Vigor returned fire. A bullet struck Roszko's hand and another ripped through his thigh. Limping and bloody, Roszko retreated into the shadows of the Quonset.

Hoogestraat gunned an RCMP truck, tires spinning in the snowy grass, and parked it across the open door.

Did you get him, Hoogestraat asked his partner.

I'm not sure, Vigor answered.

Hoogestraat yelled for Roszko to surrender. The only response was his own voice coming from the radios strapped to the officers on the floor inside.

It was quiet again.

***

James Roszko hated cops. They'd been harassing him ever since he was a teenager. Every officer who passed through the Mayerthorpe detachment knew him as a temperamental, violent man obsessed with guns whom locals called the town nutcase. Roszko scared the people he passed on the streets of Mayerthorpe. No one knew what he might do. Scream at them over some minor or imagined insult? Chase them with his truck? He'd spent little time in jail because he bullied witnesses until they declined to testify.

Besides the young men he invited to smoke marijuana and help with odd jobs, no one visited Roszko's farm. There was a steel gate across his driveway with a No Trespassing sign hung on the rails. A government employee registering voters for the last election flattened car tires on a spike belt laid across his driveway. There were rumours of other traps and buried guns on the property where his two huge dogs roamed.

Bailiffs Robert Parry and Mark Hnatiw knew a bit about Roszko when they went to his farm the day before the shootings. They'd heard about the spike belts. Parry decided he needed backup to repossess a truck from a man like that. He was right. As soon as they drove to the front gate, Roszko cursed them out, flipped them off, and unleashed his dogs in a sudden tantrum. He then leapt into the new white Ford pickup Parry and Hnatiw were there to seize and sped off over the field adjacent to his farm.

Well, Parry said, I'm going to call the cops.

When Mayerthorpe RCMP officers arrived to escort the bailiffs onto the property, one of them drew a gun. Hnatiw and Parry thought the police were paranoid.

For ninety minutes, Roszko drove around the rural roads in a fury. He knew this was trouble. They would go inside the Quonset. They would find the chop shop and the weed. Roszko, a convicted sexual predator, had no intention of going back to prison.

He needed to talk to his mother, who lived within sight of his property. She had always helped him out of trouble, ever since he was a kid. He called his Aunt Ann, but his mother wasn't there. He called back an hour later. There's a situation on my property, he told his aunt. I need to stash my truck. His aunt's place was forty kilometres from his own and safe enough. She said no, but he parked there anyway.

Roszko then called Shawn Hennessey at the Kal-Tire in nearby Barrhead, where he worked. The two had known each other for the last three years. They chatted at the tire shop and Hennessey sometimes helped with various jobs on Roszko's property. He also sold some of Roszko's pot for him. Perhaps he could park his truck at Hennessey's place.

"I'm leaving to go to work and I just don't have time to go home," Roszko said. "Can I leave it there?"

Hennessey saw through the lie. He knew about the late payments on the truck. "It's the bailiffs, right?"

"Well, yeah," Roszko said. "Bailiffs are looking for the truck."

"I don't want to be involved."

Roszko went to Hennessey's home that night anyway. A Luger pistol stuck out of his waistband as they sat around the kitchen table with Dennis Cheeseman, Hennessey's brother-in-law. Hennessey's wife kept their two young daughters in another part of the house, away from Roszko.

"I need that rifle," Roszko said, referring to the Winchester Hennessey's grandfather had given him years before. "Go get that rifle."

Hennessey did as he was told. Cheeseman put on gloves and placed the rifle in a pillowcase from the linen closet in the hall.

Roszko was still livid with the police. I'm going to burn down the Quonset, the pot, the truck parts, all of it, he told them.

The brothers-in-law followed Roszko to his Aunt Ann's, where he planned to leave his truck. The two waited in Hennessey's Dodge Neon while Roszko parked. Hennessey was pale.

We should leave him here, they told each other. Both of them were afraid. Roszko climbed into Hennessey's car and unleashed a profane rant against the RCMP. Cheeseman sat in the back with the rifle in the pillowcase as the three drove back to Mayerthorpe in silence. It was after midnight.

Roszko told Hennessey to pull over once they could see his property. There were lights on at Roszko's farm and headlights across the fields. Hennessey and Cheeseman watched as Roszko pulled thick socks over his boots to muffle the sound of his steps. He grabbed both guns and disappeared into the dark toward his farm without a word.

Hennessey and Cheeseman drove home and went to bed.

* * *

The Hennessey family heard radio reports about the murders of four RCMP officers the next day.

For months, terrified and paranoid, Hennessey and Cheeseman held their secret strictly among family. They never came forward, never told investigators they'd given the cop-killer a ride. Roszko killed himself that day, so perhaps police would never figure it out. Rumours were all over Barrhead, and it was hard to keep their heads down. Every night, the story led newscasts across the country. Reporters called it one of the worst crimes in Canadian history.

RCMP investigators knew Hennessey was involved. They just didn't know how. Roszko's cellphone records proved he had called Hennessey several times the night before the shootings. Officers suspected he gave Roszko a ride, but he wouldn't talk, and the family was too tight to break. Reporters questioned Hennessey when his name appeared in police search warrants, but he avoided them as stubbornly as he had the police. Hennessey was good at keeping his mouth shut.

Without any solid evidence against Hennessey, investigators grew frustrated. The slaying of four young police officers attracted lasting national attention, and Canadians everywhere questioned how the killings could have happened. The pressure was on.

Officers decided to change their angle. Hennessey was too tough to crack, but he wasn't the only one with a secret.

When twenty-one-year-old Cheeseman wasn't at work in the Sepallo Foods plant in Barrhead, he was usually watching television and smoking pot in his bedroom in Hennessey's basement. Cheeseman looked up to his brother-in-law and was a devoted, though withdrawn, brother himself. Everyone knew Cheeseman was shy and had trouble talking to women. So when a young woman's car broke down in the Sepallo parking lot in October 2006, nineteen months after the murders, his co-workers were quick to encourage him.

"Get out there, Dennis!" they said. "There's a good-looking girl there."

Cheeseman exchanged phone numbers with the woman after helping with her car. Her name was Constable Sue Marconi, but she never told him she was RCMP. Cheeseman was smitten with his new girlfriend and walked around with a smile on his face for months. Marconi played her part as she introduced Cheeseman to her friends, and eventually to RCMP officers posing as a criminal organization.

For months, undercover RCMP officers carefully choreographed their plan to make Cheeseman admit he and Hennessey had helped Roszko. Desperate for acceptance and respect, Cheeseman fell hard for the entire charade. He told the officers everything because he believed it would earn trust among his new friends.

Officers arrested Hennessey and Cheeseman in July 2007, each on four counts of murder. Two years had passed, and many Canadians assumed the story ended with Roszko, the crazed lone gunman who killed four cops and then himself. Though everyone knew there was an investigation, the charges came as a shock.

In January 2009, both men were convicted on the lesser charge of manslaughter.

Crown prosecutor Susan Hughson said the pair's crime was what they hadn't done, not what they had. Their failure to warn police of Roszko's oncoming threat led to the entire tragedy. Four deaths for lack of a phone call, she said.

"When you're in that situation, push comes to shove, you must do the right thing."

HYPNOTIZED

Vernon Elwood Booher burst through the front door of his neighbour's farm in a sweaty panic. He'd sprinted across several fields among the farms north of Mannville on that July night in 1928. Booher nearly collapsed through the front door of the home and startled Alex Ross and his family as they ate supper.

"Someone has shot Mother and Fred!" Booher yelled.

The twenty-two-year-old bolted out the door as quickly as he'd arrived, leaving the confused Ross family to call Mannville's doctor and the nearest Alberta Provincial Police detachment in Vermilion.

The Ross family felt ill. They'd heard gunshots from the Booher residence earlier that night and thought nothing of it. Gunshots to scare foxes away from chicken coops were common in the area.

Booher was back on his family farm by the time Dr. Joseph Heaslip arrived. He was calm, but still heaved for breath when he met the doctor at the gate. The family dog barked at the doctor as Booher gestured toward the house.

"They are all dead up there," he said.

Booher led the doctor into the family home by the light of a lit match.

Vernon's mother, Eunice, was dead at her dining room table. She'd been seated when a bullet entered the back of her skull and shattered a bowl of strawberries on the table in front of her. Her arms were now outstretched on the wooden tabletop amid a mess of blood, pulp, and seeds. The forty-four-year-old mother of four was preparing dinner when she was killed. There was a pie ready on the kitchen counter, and tea and rice boiled on the stove.

Fred, Vernon's older brother by two years, was dead on the kitchen floor. He'd been shot twice in the head, once in the front and again in the back.

In the flickering light, it took only moments for Heaslip to confirm the two were dead. The doctor took Vernon Booher back outside.

Henry, the father of the family, was not at home. He'd spent the day working his fields on land nearly ten kilometres away and wasn't expected home that night. The two youngest children, both daughters, spent the evening at their basketball practice in Mannville.

Vernon was alone in the pasture with the cows earlier that evening, he said. He heard shots before suppertime, but thought Fred or a hired hand had shot at an animal that had come too close to the yard. Eunice and Fred were dead when he returned home for supper shortly after, Vernon told the doctor. He hadn't seen either of the farm's hired hands since.

Booher and Heaslip waited tensely for police in the farmyard, perched upon a hill over the Vermilion river valley eighty kilometres west of the Saskatchewan border. The highway was only forty feet from the front step. The Boohers had moved from Oklahoma to Alberta for cheap land ten years before and had lived near Mannville for the last four.

Desperate for distraction, Booher and the doctor began to search the property. In the bunkhouse, a derelict railcar near the barn, they found Gabriel Gromley dead on the floor. The hired hand was shot twice in the face and once in the chest. The wounds were grotesque, caused by bullets bigger than any pistol could fire.

Constable Frederick Olsen, the Alberta Provincial Police officer in the Vermilion detachment, arrived in the middle of the night. Booher and Heaslip told him of the carnage they'd found. Booher was calm for someone who'd spent the evening stumbling over corpses, Olsen thought.

They found Bill dead ten feet inside the barn door. Booher didn't even know the young Ukrainian's last name. The hired man was face down on the floor with a gunshot wound in the back of his head. The slop bucket he carried was spilled on the floor beside him.

With Bill dead, everyone was accounted for except the killer.

Olsen was confused. The idea that a stranger walked onto the farm and killed anyone he or she saw was terrifying. Surely the work of some sort of lunatic. Although, would someone so crazed have thought to collect the rifle shells after killing? Olsen hadn't spotted any as he scoured the farm.

The Booher farm had two rifles, both still on a rack at the back door of the house. Olsen disregarded both of them as the murder weapon because they were dusty from lack of use. As he searched through the night, Olsen finally found a rifle shell in the pot of rice on the stove. It was dumb luck that a shell was hidden near Fred Booher's body and provided Olsen with a key clue.

It was a powerful .303-calibre shell. Such big rifles were rare around Mannville, Olsen knew, which would make the murder weapon easier to find.

At sunrise, Olsen drove to Mannville to call for assistance from the Alberta Provincial Police headquarters in Edmonton. The crime was bigger than one man could handle.

Olsen took Booher with him. They would need the calm young man as a material witness, and the detectives from Edmonton would be eager to speak to him when they arrived. It was routine to keep such a witness close, and Olsen took Booher to the Mannville Fire Hall so they could rest.

Booher stayed near the stove. Before he fell asleep, he muttered to himself, "I don't know why the deuce I ever did it."

Olsen overheard and asked what he meant.

Booher didn't answer.

The next day, July 10, 1928, the murders were all Mannville talked about. The popular theory was that some vile stranger had wandered into their midst, because no local could be so cold-blooded.

Poor Vernon, many said, to discover his mother and brother like that. Booher, known as Bunny, was a good-looking young man and Mannville's best hockey player. It was such a shame.

Detective Sergeant Frank Leslie arrived from Edmonton to lead the investigation. He sent officers to the Booher farm while he viewed the four bodies in Mannville.

In the morning light, as neighbours tried to scrub the bloodstains clean inside the Booher house, officers searched for clues. Particularly, they wanted to find the rifle. Police wondered if the killer had tossed the weapon into the Vermilion River, a short walk from the farmhouse.

The only person near Mannville who owned a .303-calibre rifle was Charles Stephenson, who'd lived for decades on a nearby farm. Stephenson told police he'd lent his old British Army rifle to the Booher family months before. He was certain it was since returned but couldn't find the rifle in his home. A box of shells was also missing. Stephenson had been home with his family that evening and wasn't a suspect.

In the day after the murders, police repeatedly questioned Booher about any details he might have missed or forgotten. The cops broke off their questions when Vernon's father, Henry, came to visit his surviving son at the fire hall. Leslie would take him to Edmonton tomorrow, his father said, and it was best that he went. Henry Booher was haggard and slumped during the short visit.

"If I had known the old man would take it that hard," Vernon said once his father left, "it would never have occurred."

Officers in the room questioned Booher. What wouldn't have occurred?

Booher didn't answer.

The case stagnated for more than a week. Officers didn't find Stephenson's .303 rifle or any other. No murderous stranger was found wandering central Alberta. No guilty conscience came forward. No one imagined any motive that could explain why Eunice Booher, her son Fred, and two random hired hands were gunned down.

Booher stuck to his story. The problem was no one could substantiate much of that story until Booher reached the Ross home for help. Police at least found someone who could corroborate the beginning.

Around 6:30 the evening of the murders, Manville town councillor Will Scott arrived at the Booher farm to drop off a tax receipt. Vernon met him at the gate. They chatted for a few minutes and nothing appeared to be wrong. Bill, whose last name turned out to be Rosyak, walked toward the farmhouse behind the two men. Booher snapped at him to feed the pigs instead of going inside the house. Bill turned and headed for the slop bucket later found by his body.

Olsen and Leslie hadn't forgotten about Booher's strange mutterings in the hours after the killings. Both thought he was guilty and were desperate to prove it when a bizarre solution called from Vancouver.

On the other end of the line was Dr. Adolph Maximilian Langsner, a noted criminologist originally from Vienna, Austria. Langsner was famous for his claim that he could read minds. The thirty-five-year-old had studied applied psychology in France and was since said to have used his unique skills to crack a ring of pirates in China, identify a jewel thief in Germany, and catch an arsonist in Romania. Langsner told the Alberta officers he would help solve the Booher case for $250. He happened to be visiting Canada and read about the killings in the newspaper.

The Alberta Provincial Police were sceptical, but Langsner had recently consulted for Vancouver police and taught some of their officers hypnosis. He possessed some legitimacy.

Leslie accepted Langsner's help, but did not wait for it. The officer charged Booher with four murders in the hours after the phone call, the day before the doctor arrived in Edmonton.

Langsner first studied Booher from across a crowded courtroom during the preliminary hearing on July 19. Through the proceedings, Langsner picked out the missing rifle as the key lack of evidence in the case. The next day, he visited Booher in his basement cell at the Fort Saskatchewan Jail. They spoke alone briefly, and then Langsner went to the Booher farm with several officers.

After what the officers thought was several minutes of aimless wandering, Langsner stooped in some tall grass and stood up with Stephenson's .303 rifle. Police were astonished the rifle was only two hundred yards from the Booher home. Though ten days of exposure had worn away any evidence, officers had their murder weapon.

Police hurried back to the basement of the Fort Saskatchewan Jail to confront Booher with the rifle. Still, he admitted nothing. Eventually, police left Langsner and Booher alone in the cell for more than an hour.

He has something to say to you, Langsner told officers once he stepped outside.

Leslie went inside the cell and listened to Booher spill.

"I want to get it all over with. I don't care if I'm hanged tomorrow," Booher said. "I killed Mother as she sat at the table and then shot my brother Fred as he rushed into the house to see what was happening.

"The two of them were lying in the house when Councillor Scott entered the yard. I don't know what I would have done, if he had attempted to enter the house.

"When Bill came in from the field, I shot him in the barn so he would not find the other bodies. Gabriel Gromley, I shot in the bunkhouse. I had planned to sink his body in fifteen feet of water and throw the rifle after him, but I didn't have time.

"I am making this confession because I want to get it over with and I don't want Father and my sisters to have to appear in court."

Police realized how close Booher came to getting away with it. Had he managed to sink Gromley's body, police would've believed the hired hand had fled.

The outcome of Booher's September 1928 trial was considered a foregone conclusion until he sent whispers through the Edmonton courtroom when he pleaded not guilty on the first day.

Booher's lawyers argued his jailhouse confession should be stricken from evidence and hidden from the jury. The mysterious Langsner obviously coerced the confession with hypnosis, they argued.

Ridiculous, the prosecutors said.

Chief Justice William Simmons ruled the confession was inadmissible because Langsner was left alone with Booher. Prosecutors could not prove hypnosis hadn't been used as coercion.

A second confession was nearly lost the next day when Thomas Stewart, a spiritual advisor from the Salvation Army, refused to testify about conversations with Booher in his cell. The courtroom went silent as Simmons stared at the man on his witness stand.

"Judas betrayed his master, and if I betray this boy, I will also betray my master," Stewart said.

Simmons was hesitant, but decided that forcing Stewart to talk was in the public interest, if unseemly.

"If I am wrong in my view, the appeal court will rectify it," Simmons said.

Booher leapt to his feet in the prisoner's box and called his lawyer over. He whispered a few words in his ear and sunk back to his seat.

"My lord," the lawyer said, "the accused desires Stewart to give the required evidence."

Thus released from his responsibility for confidentiality, Stewart told the court of his two visits with Booher for spiritual counsel in his cell.

"You have read what the papers have said about the deed?" Booher asked him.

"Yes."

Booher looked directly at Stewart. "Do you think God can forgive me for my deed?"

"Any sinner will be forgiven if he truly repents."

Stewart testified that although Booher didn't specify the deed he wanted absolution for, he believed the young man spoke of the four murders. Booher claimed to have no memory of that deadly evening, Stewart testified.

Witnesses told court they remembered seeing Booher on horseback the day before the murders, headed to the Stephenson farm nine kilometres from his own.

Booher did himself few favours when he took the witness stand. Newspaper reporters called him "impersonal and detached" as he denied the murders.

However, the court learned a possible motive from his cold testimony. Booher said there was "continual friction and unpleasantness" between him and his mother over a girl he fancied. She was a nurse at the small Mannville Hospital. Booher admitted he'd faked fainting spells and work injuries to get out of chores and spend time with her. He'd fought with his brother, Fred, about his excuses to skip farm work, Booher said.

It took the jury less than two hours to find Booher guilty. His hanging was set for December.

"Have you anything you wish to say?" Simmons asked him.

"Only that I am not guilty," Booher replied.

His conviction was overturned by the appeal court a month before he was scheduled to hang, on the grounds that prosecutors unfairly influenced the jury by referring to Booher's inadmissible first confession to Langsner in their presence. Booher was granted a new trial.

The second trial went even worse for Booher. The confession to Langsner was accepted as evidence. Better-prepared prosecutors provided experts to testify that Booher could not have been hypnotized.

This time, the hanging date was set for April 24, 1929.

"I have made my peace with God," Booher told Stewart a day before his death. "I am ready to go."

At dawn, Booher walked calmly up the gallows stairs on his own. He showed no trace of fear or remorse.

"Tremendous nerve," the hangman told him.

IN THE ROUGH

Frank Willey's disappearance started with a set of golf clubs.

As golf season approached in April 1962, the pro at Edmonton's Riverside Municipal Golf Club received a weird delivery order. The man on the phone told Willey he wanted a set of women's clubs delivered to his home as a surprise for his wife's birthday. The caller didn't care what kind as long as they were under $225. He wanted them delivered to a new home in east Edmonton in a few days, on April 19. Bring them late in the evening, the caller said, past your business hours. The man said he'd recently moved from British Columbia where a golfer had recommended the forty-eight-year-old Willey, who'd moved from Vancouver a decade before when the Riverside course opened.

The day of the delivery, Willey worked a busy eight hours at the club's pro shop. As the Easter weekend approached, golfers in the winter city were eager to tee off after months away from the links. His shop had done healthy business that year, around $25,000 in sales before the season started. He put the women's clubs into his trunk and went home for supper with his wife, Paris, and his visiting mother and sister. At around 9:30, he left to deliver the golf clubs, and was never seen again.

The golfer's fate was sealed twelve hours earlier by three men sitting at a table in Edmonton's Riviera Hotel restaurant. Raymond Daniel Workman was in a foul mood as he sipped a cup of coffee. The lean, balding accountant was already out on bail in connection with charges of counselling perjury and obstructing justice connected to a client's stolen documents, and now he wouldn't shut up about another planned crime. The forty-four-year-old wanted to hurt Frank Willey. He wanted him dead.

Across the table, Paul Osborne was uneasy. The failed salesman from eastern Canada had recently moved to Edmonton for a fresh start. He'd severed all ties, changed his name, and left the former Paul Hadley behind. After months in Edmonton, he was still unemployed and hadn't done much of anything. His fresh start had yet to begin.

"Workman was still talking about working this guy over," Osborne would later say. "He said he wanted him knocked off. He wanted him killed."

Workman wanted Osborne and the third man, William Huculak, to do the dirty work. Huculak didn't object. Thin as a rail with dark greased hair, he was a pool shark and known as Headball in Edmonton's billiard halls.

Workman wanted to make it look like an accident. They would grab Willey, take him outside the city, and run him over with a car on a country road. If they propped his body against his own car, it would appear he'd been struck while changing a flat tire. Workman thought the plan was genius.

Osborne, on the other hand, found the whole thing ridiculous and had no idea who the intended victim was. He didn't know about Workman's year-long intimate relationship with Paris, the golf professional's wife.

Workman had moved to Edmonton in September 1960 to meet more accounting clients. He lived with a local family, the Plawiuks, who were also friends of the Willeys. Irene Plawiuk considered him a moody, sullen man with a quick temper. Still, Paris visited him at her house two or three times a week.

After many visits from Paris, Workman questioned a lawyer he knew about divorce and shared property. The two men were at a business meeting in a bowling alley, and Workman approached the lawyer when it was over.

"He said he wanted information for a friend," Frank Pawlowski remembered. "He said the friend wanted to get a divorce and wondered if the friend would get most of the property of the other party."

When Workman said there was no adultery involved, Pawlowski replied it was doubtful his friend would get much property in a divorce. The lawyer thought Workman's reaction to the news seemed grim and dour.

There's no way for your friend to make this work, Pawlowski told him.

"Yes, there is," Workman said. "We'll just have to kill him."

Pawlowski gave him a shocked look.

"Forget it. Forget it," Workman quickly said. "I didn't say anything to you. Remember, you're a lawyer."

Pawlowski knew no client privilege actually protected the conversation. He wasn't Workman's lawyer.

In July 1961, Alfred Willey found himself at a Vancouver racetrack with Workman and Paris, his sister-in-law. He didn't like what he was hearing from the couple, namely that Paris intended to divorce his brother and marry Workman. He remembered how she'd been hanging all over Workman and kissing him.

Workman told his own friends and family he would marry Paris after she divorced Frank. By then, she'd filed separation papers and the legal back and forth was still ongoing nearly nine months later, when Willey disappeared.

As the men finished coffee, Osborne told them he would think about their plan. He only said it to get them off his back. The unemployed salesman wanted nothing to do with Workman's murderous personal vendetta, but Workman was persistent. He called Osborne later that afternoon, pressuring him to join the scheme.

"Is your decision final?" Workman pressed.

"Absolutely," Osborne replied, and hung up.

Workman called back around ten o'clock that night. There was stress in his voice, and he stumbled over his words.

"Everything went haywire," he told Osborne.

"You don't mean to tell me that you went through with that thing?"

"Yes," Workman went on. "It got all screwed up."

Osborne went around the corner to Huculak's downtown home and chatted with his wife while they waited for the pair to return. At 3:00 a.m., they finally arrived, shoes caked in fresh mud. Workman was ornery as usual, but Huculak was pale and twitchy instead of his smooth self. Osborne took him to the bathroom to calm him down.

"He kept saying this guy's eyes were sticking out of his head and something was sticking out the back of his head," Osborne later testified. "I realized then that it was no joke."

Huculak told Osborne they'd left a body in a shed and still needed to bury it outside the city.

His loose lips kept flapping through the entire Easter weekend. He told Osborne they later tried to bury the golfer but couldn't dig deep enough because the spring ground was still frozen.

Two days after Willey went missing, Workman backed a rented 1962 white Pontiac into Osborne's driveway. Workman insisted the wide trunk reeked and needed washing. Osborne couldn't smell anything, but he hosed down the back of the car anyway. Workman then asked Osborne to go for a drive. They drove south out of Edmonton and turned onto a country road. Workman told Osborne to drop him off, drive around for twenty minutes, then return and pick him up. Osborne didn't ask questions. At this point, he knew a man had been murdered and was frightened his silence had become criminal.

Meanwhile, the police were investigating Willey's disappearance after his sister reported him missing. The same day Osborne drove Workman to the country, officers found Willey's car parked at the curb in an east Edmonton neighbourhood undergoing construction. The women's golf clubs he'd intended to deliver were in the back seat, covered with blood.

Investigators soon ventured outside the city, concentrating on farmland near the hamlet of Looma, twenty-four kilometres southeast of Edmonton. Their first break came when Rosie Fuhrov told them two men woke her up when they knocked on her door the night Willey disappeared. They told her their car was stuck in a muddy field nearby and asked to borrow a shovel.

At the next farm, investigators spoke to Wilburt Crosswhite. The same two men who'd called on Rosie Fuhrov knocked on his door an hour later, asking for help to get their car unstuck. Crosswhite pulled Workman's rental car out of the mud with his truck, breaking one of the white Pontiac's taillight in the process.

Detective John Evans found a fragment of the broken tail light in the muddy field and matched it to Workman's rental car. Workman returned the Pontiac to an Edmonton Avis outlet with more than seventeen hundred kilometres on the odometer. The rear bumper was damaged, the trunk mats were missing, and the car was littered with soiled rags.

"Workman told me he had spilled paint in the trunk and he wished to clean it," rental agent Fernand Gibeau told police.

The car stunk of cleaning solvent when Evans inspected it. He discovered hairs that matched samples collected from Willey's golf caps.

As the investigation continued, Paris took over her missing husband's pro shop at the golf course. Workman drove the golfer's mother and sister to visit family in Lacombe in Willey's own car. They believed he was a friend of the family.

In early May, two weeks after Willey vanished, Workman and Huculak were charged with murder despite the lack of a body. Workman was arrested in Edmonton and Huculak a few days later on an eastbound passenger train in Orillia, Ontario.

Workman admitted nothing. He had an explanation for every piece of evidence detectives threw at him. The heavy mileage on his rental car was all from legitimate business travel around Edmonton, he said. Workman claimed he'd been at a friend's house the night the golfer disappeared.

He'd watched a hockey game, drunk beer, and fallen asleep in front of the television. Around midnight, he woke up and went to his new apartment. Officers knew he was lying. Workman's landlady had already told them he hadn't arrived home until midafternoon the next day. He left a trail of mud through the halls, she remembered.

As the interview ended, police bluntly accused Workman of murder, and he leapt angrily to his feet.

"You're trying to implicate me in something I know nothing about," he yelled.

In September 1962, people lined the corridors of Edmonton's courthouse for a chance to observe the trial. When one spectator in the gallery tired and left, another quickly filled the seat.

Prosecutors painted the jury a picture of Willey's last moments. Huculak had escorted him into the partially constructed home when he arrived to deliver the golf clubs. Workman then ambushed Willey inside the house, and they both dragged the golfer to the basement. They taped a cloth around a steel wrench, then used it to knock him unconscious for the drive out of Edmonton to stage his "accidental" death. During the attack, the cloth fell off and Willey suffered a severe head injury when the steel struck his skull. Later, investigators found a pool of blood on the concrete floor and tape wrapped around a loose cloth nearby.

Frank Lieber, Workman's lawyer, said the prosecution's story was an overblown theory that didn't match the motive.

"Really, gentlemen," he asked the jury, "do you have to kill to get a man's wife?"

The jury took two hours and twenty-six minutes to agree Workman did just that. He and Huculak were sentenced to hang, a sentence later commuted to life in prison by the federal Progressive Conservative government in 1963.

Willey's body was never found.

HOLLYWOOD SCRIPT

Dennis Kim and his cousins, the Bai brothers, thought a bank robbery should be done with style. None of them had any experience in thievery, but they'd watched a lot of creative plots orchestrated in Hollywood movies. To Kim, a bank robbery was a good trick, a magician's sleight of hand that fooled people as well as stole from them. Such a robbery wasn't easy to put together. It took Kim and his cousins nine months of meticulous thought to plan the August 2006 robbery of the CIBC branch in the mountain town of Banff.

The plan started in late 2005, when Kim offered friends and family a role in his grand plan. He needed two accomplices, he told them. Kim had already picked a date and authored scripts for what each of the robbers would say. In his Vancouver home, Kim's desk was covered with maps of Banff and blueprints of the CIBC branch at the corner of Banff Avenue and Buffalo Street. Several people turned Kim down before his cousins agreed to help.

Ronald Bai knew the bank in downtown Banff well. He'd quit his job there only six months before. Ronald and his brother Roy had grown up in the tourist town and knew every street. They were perfect for Kim's plan.

For months, they worked out the details amidst gaps in their private lives. Kim was a computer science student in Vancouver, while the Bai brothers now lived in Calgary.

They decided to hit the bank during daylight. A subtle break-in wasn't what Kim wanted.

As the day approached, Kim called one of his professors to reschedule an exam that conflicted with the robbery. Then, he and the Bais met in a Canmore hotel room twenty-six kilometres from Banff.

On the afternoon of August 8, they drove from Canmore and stopped at a cluster of pay phones inside the Banff Centre, a conference building several blocks from the bank. Kim had long planned to pull the robbery on this specific day, a particularly busy one in the narrow, crowded streets of Banff. The town was hosting an international golf tournament at the Banff Springs Hotel, and professionals Jack Nicklaus, Greg Norman, and John Daly were on the links with more than $350,000 in winnings at stake. In addition to the town's usual tourist rush, the second day of the tournament brought more media, golf fans, and sightseers.

The men set their plan in motion with three phone calls at 3:30 p.m.

They called 911 from the Banff Centre and hung up without a word.

In a second 911 call, they told the operator a drunk man with a gun was inside the Banff Springs Hotel at the south end of town.

There's a bomb in a suitcase in your hotel that will explode at 4:30 p.m., they told the woman who answered the phone at the Rimrock Resort Hotel, even further south. There were more than three hundred people inside the Rimrock when the call came in.

"A lot of people are going to die," Kim told the front-desk attendant as he read from his script.

The calls sent the small Banff RCMP detachment into disarray, and officers raced south as Kim and the Bais headed north to the CIBC.

Twenty minutes later, just before the bank closed, the three men strode through the front doors and pulled on black balaclavas as they walked downstairs to the commercial accounts department. There were fewer security measures downstairs than at the commonly used tellers on the ground floor.

One of the black masks turned to a man and his three-year-old son, the only customers in the bank. They pointed replica handguns at the father and son and told them to get on the floor.

They then turned their guns toward Chantal Campo behind the main counter and ordered her to deactivate an alarmed door and get down. As she laid on the tiles, all Campo could think about was whether she'd ever see her two boys again. They were too young to be without a mother, she thought. She was terrified.

Kim and the Bais made the clerks start the door timers on the vaults. They couldn't be opened for at least five minutes, and then only in a thirty-second window with the right keys. It was the same procedure Ronald Bai had learned when he worked there.

The first employee they asked for the keys tearfully said she didn't have them.

"If she is fucking lying to us," Kim said loudly, "I'm going to slit her throat."

As the timers ticked down, another two bank employees walked downstairs and came face to face with the three guns.

They were secured roughly at the ankles and wrists with plastic zip ties.

"This is going to hurt," they were told as the plastic cut into their wrists.

The seconds ticked by. Seven bank employees, one father, and one child lay on the floor. Outside the bank, people strolled by with no idea what was going on inside. No one triggered any alarms.

One of the Bai brothers kneeled next to a male employee. "Do you want me to rape these girls in front of you here? Close your eyes."

Once the vault doors opened, the robbers divided stacks of cash into three backpacks that would blend in with the many others hung over shoulders in the mountain town.

The three of them collected $337,246 in American and Canadian currency less than a half-hour after they arrived.

Kim and his cousins dropped four smoke grenades in the bank and escaped through thick red clouds. The trio had practiced setting off the grenades weeks before at a construction site in Burnaby. They'd even videotaped themselves as they discussed how many grenades they'd need and whether the smoke could be fatal. Inside the bank, the hostages' relief turned to fear that the building was on fire.

The three men disappeared onto the crowded sidewalks and eventually drove north out of Banff while police were frantic in the south. Firefighters discovered the robbery when they arrived at the bank and found smoke grenades instead of flames.

Officers abandoned their search for an imaginary bomb at the Rimrock Hotel. Off-duty officers were called for work and left the golf crowds, trading polo shirts for their uniforms.

The three robbers returned to their Canmore hotel long before the RCMP pieced it all together. The next day, Kim escaped back to British Columbia and the brothers went home to Calgary.

"They were good operators," RCMP Corporal Scott Fuller said. He'd quickly connected the fake phone calls to the bank robbery. "It's too convenient for all that to be going on at once. It's not your run-of-the-mill bank robbery."

RCMP considered the possibility of an inside man only hours into the investigation. The robbers they watched on security footage knew the bank too well for average thieves, even ones who'd been inside as customers. Eventually, the trail led to former employees and then to Ronald Bai. Friends told investigators about Kim's attempts to recruit them.

Weeks after the robbery, on September 15, the RCMP raided Kim's home. They seized a replica handgun, $80,000 in cash, and the video of the men practicing with the smoke grenades. Ronald Bai was arrested in Calgary the next day.

Apprehending Roy Bai took longer. The older brother moved to South Korea shortly after the robbery. Even when RCMP found him, it wasn't easy to get him back to Calgary. After a long negotiation between Mounties, lawyers, Bai, and his family, he returned to Canada and was arrested at the Vancouver International Airport eight weeks after the robbery.

All three pleaded guilty in a Calgary courtroom months later.

"I made a very terrible mistake that day," Kim told his former hostages in the court gallery.

At sentencing, Court of Queen's Bench Justice Beth Hughes focused on the bank job's elaborate plan. "In my time on the bench here, I haven't seen another robbery with this level of sophistication. It can only be described as exceedingly sophisticated, organized, and well-planned out."

Defence lawyer Balfour Der told the judge the three robbers were not true criminals, just young men acting out a fantasy.

"We will never see them here again," the lawyer said. The plan came about only because his clients were "watching too many movies and watching too much television."

LESS THAN TWENTY
DOLLARS OF GAS

Linda Marie Bowen waited nervously behind the wheel of her Oldsmobile Delta 88 for her son to meet her at the rendezvous. After midnight, the dim parking lot of the Food For Less in northwest Calgary was deserted. Andrew would show up, she told herself as she waited between the pale yellow pools of the lampposts. They were in this together. Surely, nothing bad could happen with such a simple plan.

The mother and son were in Calgary to steal. The pair had first studied a Texaco gas station as a potential target, but gave up when the attendant locked the door and turned the lights out while they watched from across the street. They quickly picked another, an isolated Budget Gas station, and decided Andrew would pull off the actual robbery. He had the shotgun, a Winchester Defender twelve-gauge with a Calgary Flames sticker on the stock. It was new, bought at a Canadian Tire outlet only six weeks before. They'd told the clerk they needed the weapon to shoot magpies, but then bought the shotgun with the largest ammunition capacity and the shortest barrel. The $280 Winchester was popular among fishermen and hunters who might come across a bear.

At the time, they could still afford to buy things. Andrew Harold Kay, bearing his long-gone father's name, and his mother were about to lose their jobs at the Voyageur in

Crossfield, the closest town to the family farm. He washed dishes in the back while she waitressed tables out front. They were at least $5,000 in debt in January of 1987, perhaps twice that. They were behind on the bills and the monthly $350 rent on the farmhouse. Lately, she and Andrew paid for groceries in Crossfield with rolls of the quarters her customer left as tips on the Voyageur tables. They couldn't afford to do much in their spare time. Linda would sit in Loretta's Cafe, sip endless cups of coffee, and watch shy, quiet Andrew shoot pool. At their farm, the mother and son shared a bedroom.

Before her tense wait at the rendezvous, Linda watched from a hotel parking lot as Andrew pulled away from the Budget station robbery in the 1984 black Ford Ranger he'd stolen from outside a Red Deer bank two days before. They'd switched the licence plates with those of another random truck when they arrived in Calgary that morning. She'd kept the Oldsmobile in park for ten minutes to see if cops would arrive, then headed to the Food For Less and waited.

Andrew didn't get out of the stolen truck when he pulled into the parking lot. Through the vehicle windows, she watched her son, with his shaggy hair and teenage features on his twenty-one-year-old face, desperately gesture for her to follow him. Worried, she tailed him to another empty parking lot at Sunridge Mall.

"What's wrong?" she asked him.

"I shot him."

"You couldn't have done that." She thought he meant the gas station attendant. She would've heard the gunshot as she kept watch from the hotel parking lot. "Why?"

"Because he shot back," Andrew said. "God, I shot a cop."

They wiped down the stolen Ford Ranger with ammonia to eliminate fingerprints and abandoned the vehicle in the parking lot with the keys on the seat. There were six bullet holes in the driver's side.

The two drove aimlessly around Calgary in the Oldsmobile for most of the night. Near dawn, they eventually stopped across the city at a sandwich shop and ordered sodas. Andrew told his mother what had happened.

The Budget gas station was closing for the night as he arrived, so Andrew decided not to go inside and take the register. Instead, he sped away with a tank of stolen gas worth $19.26. The attendant called the police, reported the theft, and gave a description of the truck. The thief wore a dark ball cap, the attendant said.

Nearby, at the Calgary International Airport, RCMP Constable Gordon Kowalczyk was on duty and heard the theft call come over the radio. Kowalczyk had been a Mountie eleven years and worked out of the airport detachment. The thirty-five-year-old had recently remarried and was a father of three young children. Airport staff affectionately called him the Polish Prince.

Alone in his cruiser, Kowalczyk quickly spotted a truck that fit the description on the periphery of airport property and followed it along a dark, deserted service road. On his radio, he told fellow officers he was going to pull the truck over.

Flashlight in hand, Kowalczyk approached the driver's side of the truck on foot and was met by a shotgun blast from inside the cab. Later, investigators concluded the officer emptied his gun into the side of the truck as he lay bloodied on the frigid road. Andrew fired back three times through the door. The driver's side window shattered. Andrew could have floored the gas pedal and sped away from the officer. The badly wounded Kowalczyk could have done nothing to stop him.

Instead, Andrew stepped outside the truck and blasted the officer twice more at point-blank range in a cold execution. He stole the Mountie's empty .38-calibre Smith and Wesson revolver. Kowalczyk was dead before Andrew jumped back into the truck and sped away to meet his mother.

Constable Doug Marshinew had been in contact over the radio with Kowalczyk as they searched for the truck. Marshinew heard his fellow officer say he'd found a suspect vehicle, but now couldn't reach him on the radio. Marshinew's stomach turned.

An airport employee on the way home from the night shift found Kowalczyk on the road five kilometres north of Calgary's city limits. The employee used the officer's own radio to call for help.

"There's a policeman lying in the middle of the road and I think he's dead."

Marshinew heard the call and was the first officer to find his fellow Mountie on the road. When more investigators arrived and lit the area with spotlights, they found shotgun casings and a black Quaker State ball cap in the snow. Hours later, they found the stolen truck with the bullet holes in the Sunridge Mall parking lot. Andrew Kay and his mother were gone.

Kowalczyk's funeral was held later that week. More than fifteen hundred people attended, a third of them police officers from across Canada.

Around the same time, the terrified mother and son stood on the snowy banks of the Oldman River near Lethbridge. They tossed Kowalczyk's revolver into the cold water. Linda then went to the graves of her parents near Lethbridge and confessed Kowalczyk's killing to the ground where they were buried.

"I went and told my mom and dad we were sorry," she later told police. "I had to talk to somebody."

They then returned home and waited. They nervously watched the nightly news coverage of the killing and investigation that turned up no solid leads for weeks.

The pair lived on the rented farm near Crossfield, fifty kilometres north of Calgary, with a menagerie of animals—five goats, six dogs, and twenty cats. The family had sold their horses months earlier to help pay the bills. Linda Bowen, a short woman with greying hair and large eyeglasses, had lived with Andrew and her older son, Michael, for thirteen years since their father left and stayed gone.

Linda and Andrew had gained no new respect for the law with the death of Kowalczyk. They'd been busy with more thefts and had robbed two convenience stores in Calgary and two restaurants in Edmonton, including a Boston Pizza.

On February 22, 1987, assistant manager Peter Falkenau was at the northeast Edmonton Boston Pizza's cash register when Linda approached him and showed him the revolver in her hand.

"She had a blank look on her face," Falkenau recalled. "She said, 'Give me the money. All of it. Now.'"

As Linda fled with $700 in cash, Falkenau yelled at customers to get the licence plate of her getaway vehicle. A few customers followed her outside, but scattered when Andrew stepped out of the Oldsmobile and fired the shotgun into the air. They sped away, but one customer managed to memorize their licence plate. A shell casing found in the parking lot by police matched the ones scattered beside Kowalczyk's body weeks before.

The next night, the RCMP went to the farm outside Crossfield in force. The family was watching David Letterman on television when the dogs began barking outside. Andrew grabbed a flashlight and went outside to investigate. Tactical officers ordered him to give up and fired two warning shots over his head.

"Don't shoot," he called into the darkness. "Don't shoot."

The officers lobbed tear gas into the house before they stormed inside. With red eyes, Linda emerged from the clouded home in handcuffs.

Fifteen officers scoured the farm for evidence of their fellow officer's murder. The loaded shotgun with the Calgary Flames sticker was found in a freezer in the house. The registration card from the stolen, bullet-marked truck was under the spare wheel well in the trunk of the family's Oldsmobile. Police found the fake handgun Linda had used in the Boston Pizza holdup.

"Be a man," Corporal Al MacIntyre told Andrew during an early police interview. "Be upfront about it."

Andrew sat sullenly and admitted nothing.

"No comment until I see a lawyer," he said.

"His attitude never changed," MacIntyre later testified. "He was indifferent to us, sort of carefree. He didn't have any concerns."

When Linda talked, police recorded every word. She said everything. My son only killed that officer because he was scared, she said. It wouldn't have happened if she'd been there.

"I wouldn't have let him, just like I wouldn't have shot anybody. I wouldn't have let him shoot a policeman if it meant me going up for murder."

She wept through most of the six-hour interview. "I just hung my son. I just hung my son. Being with me is just getting the poor kid into trouble."

They were both charged with first-degree murder and four armed robberies. Both were denied bail.

Four weeks into their joint trial, after her wide-ranging interview with investigators was ruled admissible, Linda pleaded guilty to manslaughter. In the prisoner's box, she kissed her son as she left the courtroom with a thirteen-year sentence.

Andrew showed not even a hint of remorse and was sentenced to life.

MOVING DAY

Alfred Cecil Pearce was nervous about his family's new home in northwest Calgary. He'd bought the house only two days before, when the Pearces arrived in the city from Port Alberni, British Columbia. For decades, a series of renters had lived in the North Hill home and might not have taken care of the place, he thought. The day the family moved in, a Saturday in July 1948, Pearce got to work inspecting the six-room house. He peeled back sod and stripped baseboards to study the foundation. He walked through each room, examining everything from the door frames to the wallpaper. In one of the bedrooms, he paused. Pearce pressed his foot down harder and felt the wooden floorboards give a little under the pressure.

Annoyed, Pearce went to the kitchen and through a trap door to a small dugout cellar beneath the home. From below, he could see that two sections of floor joists beneath the bedroom's weak floor had been sawed off and removed. It was odd, Pearce thought. He could think of no reason that would justify the trouble of removing the supports. The other joists appeared to be in good shape. He went back to the bedroom and stared at the unsupported section of floor. Pearce wanted to investigate. He pried up the floorboards.

A corpse stared up at him. The mummified body was partially buried in ash, but the skull, left arm, left leg, and a portion of the torso were visible in the foot-deep grave. The body was well-preserved by the ash in the cool, dry crawl space. Some skin remained, pulled thin and tight over the dead man's forehead and cheekbones. The body was clad in a leather jacket, work pants, and a pair of wool socks. A ring with "99" engraved on it was around the pinky finger of the left hand.

There were two small holes at the left temple. A dusty envelope was covered in ash beside the body.

Pearce could now see the joists were removed to make room for the corpse. He was outraged. After he phoned the police, the father of three called the Crown Trust Housing Corporation, from whom he'd purchased the house.

You sold me a house with a dead body under the floor, he told them.

Pearce's wife was horrified and started talking about a ghost. Their three children were spooked and, after the gruesome discovery, claimed they had felt a cold, clammy hand poking them when they'd first arrived.

Inspector Reg Clements and other officers arrived shortly. They brushed away some of the ash for a better look as they studied the corpse. Clements made several quick, obvious conclusions. No one could fracture his own skull and bury himself under the floorboards.

"This is definitely a case of foul play," he said. "We can't yet say how the man died, but the circumstances point to murder."

The couple who lived in the house before the Pearce family told police they'd occasionally smelled a foul odour, but thought an animal had burrowed beneath the backyard shed and died. They'd shovelled under the shed, found nothing, and decided to live with the smell.

The dead man's clothes contained no identification, but the envelope beside him was addressed to Thomas C. Hall, from a Fred Hall in the Alberta town of High River. The postmark was nineteen years old.

A phone call to the housing corporation confirmed that sixty-six-year-old Thomas Charles Hall once lived in the home, but had disappeared in March 1929 without a word. A corporation employee found the front door open after several failed attempts to contact Hall. Assuming he was gone, they'd rented the home to someone else.

Hall had married his wife, Camilla Rose, in the United States and had two sons, Charles and Fred. Eventually, the family moved to Lethbridge where their third son, John, was born. In 1923, shortly after the Halls moved to Calgary, Camilla Rose left her husband. His three boys eventually became adults and moved out, leaving their father alone in the house on 20th Avenue.

No one had worried much when Hall vanished nineteen years before. He had no dependant family left and probably just moved. There was no police record of his death, and no missing person report was ever filed. Camilla Rose, then a waitress at the Calgary bus depot, thought he'd simply moved on. So did his youngest son, John, who went to visit his father one day and found him gone. The house was in order, with no sign of any trouble.

Long-time friend Robert Barbour had questions about Hall's disappearance, but never asked them until his body was found.

"I often in my own mind wondered why he had disappeared, but I did nothing about it as it was none of my business," he said. "I know no one who had a spite against him."

Hall was a private man. Even though they were friends for many years, Barbour never met any of his children.

Hall supported himself with odd jobs, Barbour remembered, like threshing and driving teams of horses on local farms.

Oddly, both Camilla Rose and Hall's brother Wallace remembered a 1930 Calgary newspaper article that said Hall and his son Charles were killed in an automobile accident in North Dakota. Camilla Rose knew the article was mistaken because Charles was alive and well. She had reported the false story to police and forgotten about it. To both her and Inspector Clements, the false article now seemed more ominous, perhaps placed there on purpose.

The next day, Wallace viewed the body. He saw similarities in the nose, forehead, and height and told officers the corpse was his brother. John wasn't so sure it was his father. It was the middle son, Fred, who confirmed the identity when he remembered his father's "99" ring.

A day after viewing his father's body, John was seriously injured in a plane crash at the Currie Airfield southwest of Calgary. John was test piloting a twin-engine Beechcraft for the Royal Canadian Air Force when the engine died shortly after takeoff. John managed a quick emergency landing less than a kilometre from the runway, but clipped a telephone pole on the way down. He suffered head injuries in the crash and was admitted to the Colonel Belcher Hospital.

As John recovered, Clements was busy investigating Hall's finances. He hadn't just made money on local farms. Friends and family told the officer he owned American land and oil stocks worth a lot of money. Clements discovered Hall's farm work wasn't his main source of income.

"Robbery may have been the motive, as Thomas Hall was a man who had a considerable amount of money, from time to time," the inspector said.

Still in a hospital bed, John missed his father's funeral but was released by the month's end to attend the inquest. A pathologist testified Hall was murdered before he was buried. He'd died of a head injury.

"The fracture could have been caused by one or more blows on the left side of the head by any heavy solid object applied with considerable force," Dr. Lola McLatchie said.

The official declaration of murder was the last development in Hall's case. No charges were ever filed, and the identity of the killer remains a mystery.

RUMOUR MILL

The tension was growing all afternoon in Yvonne Johnson's Wetaskiwin home as the empty alcohol bottles accumulated.

Johnson, a mother of three young children, was listening to her older cousin Shirley Anne Salmon's enthusiastic rants about how a neighbourhood acquaintance was a child molester who abused his daughter. Salmon seemed to take pure joy in the bit of unproven gossip.

Salmon had arrived unexpectedly at Johnson's home that week in September 1989 in the midst of a trip from Saskatoon to Edmonton. Salmon intended to register for a computer class in the city, but seemed in no hurry actually to get there. She was content to sit around the house, drink, and ramble endlessly. The twenty-seven-year-old Johnson didn't particularly want Salmon around the house, but she was family and the door should be open for family.

Johnson knew the man Salmon was talking about—Leonard Charles Skwarok, better known as Chuck—from the neighbourhood. He'd even been in her home chatting with Salmon earlier that afternoon. He and Johnson shared rides in Wetaskiwin from time to time. She barely knew the man, but had never heard anything about him being a danger to kids.

Skwarok was separated from his common-law wife at the time, but was still close to her family. Skwarok was a natural teacher. He taught his wife how to fix minor problems with her car, how to do basic home improvements, and how to restore old furniture, a personal hobby of his. Skwarok liked going to the Wetaskiwin dump and finding salvageable items he could polish and repair. Once, he found a broken lamp ready for garbage pickup by the curb. He took it home, fixed the wiring, and gave it to his stepdaughter for her bedroom.

Skwarok told Salmon he planned to return to Johnson's home that night to drink with them. The idea of that impending visit, when her children would be asleep, sloshed around in Johnson's stomach along with the beer and Southern Comfort she'd been drinking all afternoon. That morning, Skwarok told Salmon his wife had accused him of grabbing at their young daughter. Skwarok said it was bullshit, that he hadn't done anything. It wasn't serious. The police weren't involved or anything.

Salmon took the seed of Skwarok's miserable story and spun it into a much more sinister tale, something more fun for her. She told Johnson that Skwarok already had a court date for a charge against him. Salmon claimed he'd admitted it.

"You phone him, get him over here, I'll ask him to his face. You'll see," the thirty-nine-year-old told her cousin. "He told me. I'm not bullshitting."

Johnson called Skwarok, but handed the phone to Salmon before he picked up. He said he still planned to come over. Afterward, Johnson told Salmon to ask him about his daughter once he arrived.

Johnson worried the rumour might be true. What could she and Salmon do to protect her children? A friend, Ernie Egon Jensen, was also hanging around, fixing a freezer in the garage. A quiet man who bore burn scars from a traffic accident, he helped around the house and was friends with Dwayne Wegner, Johnson's live-in boyfriend. Johnson didn't believe Jensen would be much of a match for Skwarok if he tried something. He'd been drinking since he arrived at noon and now stumbled when he walked. Wegner would be home from work before Skwarok arrived, she hoped.

Later that evening, at the first available opportunity, the drunk Salmon gleefully told Jensen and Wegner that Johnson allowed a child molester in her house. All four of them talked about Skwarok as they drank in Johnson's living room, Salmon later testified.

"Let's do him in," Johnson said.

"Are you serious?" Salmon asked.

"Yes."

Salmon looked around the room. "Oh, Ernie won't. He'll tell."

"No I won't," Jensen said.

Salmon later admitted she knew Johnson wouldn't take accusations of child molestation lightly. She'd lived through similar tragedy. As a child, Johnson endured years of sexual abuse from the male members of her large family. The daughter of a Norwegian father and a Cree mother of the Red Pheasant First Nation in Saskatchewan, Johnson was raised south of the border in Butte, Montana.

"My father is an ex-Marine," Johnson told the government's Royal Commission on Aboriginal Peoples in April 1993. "Do you know what they do to Marines? They break them down and they take everything from them and they rebuild them into a frigging killing machine. That's what I have for a father.

"My mother was in residential school, and she told me times that they put her in a room and made her take a bath in the dark and shaved her head. And that's what I have for a mother."

At 11:00 p.m., Skwarok parked his Hornet hatchback at Johnson's small house and knocked on the front door, carrying a case of beer under his arm. Salmon let him in.

The five of them sat in the living room, drinking and talking. Johnson's children were asleep in their rooms.

"Ask him now, ask him now," Salmon mouthed to Johnson.

Jensen, Wegner, and the mother of three managed to keep their mouths shut, but Salmon could no longer contain herself.

"Tell them what you told me," she said to Skwarok. "Your wife hauled you into court, you were molesting your own girl. Tell 'em."

Skwarok stood up in anger. "I never did nothing." He stalked to the kitchen, intent on leaving the house, but never made it to the door.

Wegner and Jensen jumped Skwarok and dragged him downstairs into the home's unfinished basement, Salmon would later testify. The two women stayed upstairs and listened to the loud smacks of knuckles against flesh.

"They're beating him up pretty bad down there," Salmon said to Johnson.

The two men pummelled Skwarok with kicks and punches until he managed to pull free and scramble up the stairs.

"He was coming up the stairs trying to get away and Yvonne kicked him in the face and he went flying down," Salmon later recalled.

Johnson closed the basement door after Skwarok fell back. Wegner and Jensen took turns smashing Skwarok's head into the basement floor and then tied him to one of the basement's support posts.

"I didn't do anything," Skwarok gurgled through bloody, cracked teeth. "I didn't do anything."

Johnson pulled Skwarok's pants down and sexually assaulted him with a stool leg she brought from upstairs. She then wrapped a telephone cord around Skwarok's neck and pulled tight for fifteen seconds.

When they were finished, he no longer had a pulse.

The four went upstairs and left Skwarok on the floor while they each drank another beer. Eventually, Jensen took the body to the Wetaskiwin dump in Skwarok's own car, then parked less than a block from Johnson's house. A worker driving a garbage packer discovered Skwarok's body the next morning in the same landfill he once scoured for salvageable items to restore.

Johnson, Jensen, and Wegner were arrested shortly after the body was discovered, and Salmon was charged the next week.

In jailhouse interviews with police, Salmon admitted she'd embellished or invented everything she'd said about Skwarok. He hadn't been charged with molesting his daughter, nor admitted anything to Salmon.

"I exaggerated," Salmon told police. "I didn't mean any harm. I didn't mean anything. The thought of killing him or hurting him didn't enter my mind. I just thought the guys would just tell him to get the fuck out, if you know what's good for you."

Her mother used to exaggerate, Salmon told the officer, but she always meant well.

Salmon was sentenced to a year in prison for kicking Skwarok during the attack. Wegner and Jensen both received life sentences for second-degree murder.

In 1991, Johnson was convicted of first-degree murder with no chance of parole for twenty-five years by a Wetaskiwin jury. She served seventeen years before gaining early parole under the law's faint-hope clause.

ROAD TO RUIN

By 5:00 p.m. on January 20, 2006, Raymond Yellowknee had been free from the Peace River Correctional Centre for twelve hours and drunk for seven. Yellowknee had caught a Greyhound bus to Slave Lake that frigid morning and arrived shortly before the liquor stores opened. He drank away his first hours out of custody, as he usually had following one of his many stints in jail over the past dozen years. He'd racked up more than fifty convictions in his thirty-four years and just served a short sentence for uttering threats. He'd spent most of his adult life behind bars.

Yellowknee lurched around the Sawridge Truck Stop with the remains of a bottle of McGuinness Silk Tassel rye whisky stuck in his pocket. He searched for a ride out of town or another bottle, whichever came first. Yellowknee wanted to go north to the Wabasca reserve. It was where he'd grown up, endured his father's suicide, and sniffed his first inhalants in a life dominated by substance abuse. When he couldn't find a ride in Slave Lake, he improvised the way he knew best.

With a blood-alcohol level three times the legal limit, Yellowknee stole a white pickup truck left running outside the Frontier Fuel Distributor's office and drove west out of Slave Lake. He wasn't alone for long. Soon, the blue-and-red lights of an RCMP cruiser flashed in his rearview mirror. Yellowknee's foot stomped down on the accelerator, and the truck lurched forward on Highway 2.

* * *

West of Slave Lake, on the Driftpile First Nation reserve, the three daughters of twenty-eight-year-old Misty Chalifoux looked forward to a treat. Their mother had promised to take them to the Slave Lake Walmart to spend their allowance once she got home. Chalifoux picked up her six-month-old baby boy from her mother-in-law's after she left Northern Lakes College, where she was eighteen months away from a teaching degree.

Larissa, six years old, nearly missed the trip to spend her five dollars because she hadn't done her chores. Only a last-minute plea convinced Chalifoux to let her pile into the family's Pontiac Sunfire with her sisters—thirteen-year-old Michelle and nine-year-old Trista. Michelle wanted to be a lawyer, Trista a doctor, and Larissa told people she'd be an actress and singer.

The four of them pulled out of the driveway where the girls jumped on and off the school bus each day. They stopped for gas, and Chalifoux saw her father at the side of the road as they left the reserve. She waved, then called her husband, Sheldon, to say her father would drop by soon.

Shortly after 5:30, Chalifoux and her girls headed east on the snowy Highway 2 for the sixty-five kilometre drive to Slave Lake.

* * *

Raymond Yellowknee had a pattern that lasted most of his life. At the age of thirteen, he started to hang with a different crowd of kids and lost interest in school in favour of drinking whatever he could find and inhaling household products for cheap highs. Two years later, the grandparents who'd spoiled the boy with toys since his father's suicide sent him off the reserve to get help. He spent time in two group homes in the next five months. He did more drugs, drank more booze, and attempted to kill himself with a gun. Some nights, he would slash at himself with a knife.

As an adult, his criminal record started small with a mischief charge. Before the age of twenty, he'd also been convicted of assault with a weapon for beating an unconscious man's face to mush. In 1994, at twenty-two, he drunkenly stole his first car and sat in jail for the next six months. Only weeks after he was released, RCMP officers found Yellowknee drunk behind the wheel of another stolen vehicle.

In 1997, Yellowknee was fresh out of a stint in jail for smashing his brother-in-law's face with a hammer. The first thing he did was get drunk. Then he stole a truck near the small town of Desmerais. The RCMP quickly tracked him down, but Yellowknee never pulled over just because a cop flashed the lights and put on the sirens. Yellowknee fled the cops for fifty-eight kilometres with his speedometer red-lined at 140 kilometres an hour. He hit two oncoming vehicles, slammed into a police car, and sideswiped a minivan with four children inside. He didn't even slow down. He didn't even stop when desperate officers shot one of his tires flat. The truck's engine gave up before Yellowknee did. Later, officers would swear he deliberately tried to hit other vehicles to cause an accident that would cover his escape.

Yellowknee completed a court-ordered substance abuse program during the three-year prison term that followed. It didn't help. Once released to a halfway house, not yet off parole, he skipped an Alcoholics Anonymous meeting, and police found him drunk in a truck near Westlock, eighty-five kilometres away. Again, he sped away as police approached. Again, he was caught.

"He does not show any regard for endangering other people's lives during these high-speed chases, and obviously does not fear harming himself," a correctional officer wrote of Yellowknee at the time.

Since the day he learned to drive, the best thing anyone could say about Yellowknee's driving was that he'd never killed anyone.

* * *

Lawrence Mitchell thought it was a practical joke when his company truck pulled away from the Frontier Fuel Distributor's office in Slave Lake. When he realized it wasn't, he borrowed a co-worker's car and called police as he followed his own stolen truck. Mitchell sped behind Yellowknee onto Highway 2 at 120 kilometres an hour. Still, Yellowknee began to pull away from him.

Constables Jeffrey Schneider and Michael Taylor left the Slave Lake RCMP detachment in separate cruisers at the same time. By the time Schneider passed Mitchell on the highway in an attempt to catch Yellowknee, his speedometer was at 170 kilometres an hour. The officer's lights were bright and his sirens loud as he spotted Yellowknee and the stolen truck.

"Control, it doesn't appear he's going to stop," Schneider said into his radio.

Yellowknee sped toward a rise in the highway that bent to the left. As Schneider slowed down, he watched the stolen vehicle fishtail toward the snow in the right ditch, then overcompensate and wrench the truck left across the yellow line. Only seventeen seconds after he'd officially started his pursuit, Schneider watched the truck slam into an oncoming Pontiac Sunfire eight kilometres outside Slave Lake.

* * *

Chalifoux and her two oldest daughters were killed instantly. The youngest, Larissa, was taken by helicopter to an Edmonton hospital, where she died the next day. Word spread back along Highway 2 to the Driftpile First Nation reserve faster than official notifications.

Chalifoux's older sister, Rhonda Giroux, was hosting a youth group at a local church when she heard the news. In immediate grief, she shattered coffee pots and mugs against the walls. While Chalifoux's mother, Muriel Carifelle, wept, her father called the Slave Lake Walmart and repeatedly demanded they page his daughter. There was no answer. Sheldon was left a widower with the couple's two infant sons.

"Life has been a living nightmare since January 20, 2006—one long, continuous, living nightmare," he wrote in a victim impact statement a year later. "Does anyone even realize how devastating it is to hold a child at birth, only to lose three of them in the very same fatal instant? I never thought in my God-given life that would ever happen to me, and why?"

* * *

Yellowknee would later say he remembered nothing of the crash. He blacked out in the moment before the collision and woke in an Edmonton hospital bed with a broken neck and a police officer by his side. Months later, in court, he seemed surprised his life's pattern had finally taken a bloody toll.

"I never thought my recklessness would hurt anybody," he told a near-empty courtroom as the hum of portable heaters nearly drowned out his meek voice. "I wish that it was me instead of them. I always thought it was me that was going to end up losing my life."

The court sentenced Yellowknee to more than twenty years for the crash, the longest impaired-driving sentence in Alberta's history, and one of the most severe ever handed down in Canada.

Yellowknee only served fourteen months of his record sentence before he hung himself with a belt in a segregated cell at the Edmonton Institution.

SNOWMAN

Joseph Laboucan was bored and restless. On a Friday night at the beginning of April 2005, he was crashing in a friend's cheap room at the lime-green Windmill Motel in west Edmonton. True to its name, there was a high windmill on the parking lot sign. The surly nineteen-year-old couldn't afford a place of his own and was only in the city for a short stretch. He'd lived most of his life in Fort St. John, in the northeast corner of British Columbia, though he was trying to make Alberta's capital his new home. Bus trips and rides with friends into Alberta were common over the last two years. Laboucan spent days at the nearby West Edmonton Mall among the teenagers and drug dealers who practically lived there. They knew him as Snowman. Many of the mall rats, as they were called, gave themselves similar nicknames.

Laboucan told friends in Fort St. John he sold drugs for gangs in Alberta. He bragged about a million-dollar settlement he was getting from a car crash two years before. There was a steel plate in Laboucan's back after a trip to Edmonton ended when his friend's car flipped into the ditch alongside the highway. In the next few months, despite the plastic body cast he wore, Laboucan picked fights. He was no longer the meek follower he'd once been.

"He didn't know when to shut his mouth and leave things alone," a friend recalled. "He felt a little bit too confident with himself."

Laboucan told friends he was a new man. He was Snowman now, he said, no longer Body Cast Joe. He could tell his friends whatever stories he wanted about himself. None of them knew him well enough to dispute anything he said.

Laboucan met his ex-girlfriend Stephanie Bird and Michael Briscoe, her older boyfriend, by chance as he wandered through downtown Edmonton. They chatted for a few minutes, and Laboucan told them he had no place to live. He'd arrived with friends from Fort St. John but hadn't returned with them. They agreed to take him in once he promised them $1,000 from the upcoming settlement he mentioned.

For a week, Laboucan spent days at the mall and nights on the motel room floor. He smoked drugs, drank, and survived on hot dogs cooked in the room's small kitchenette. When the group was sick of hot dogs, they went to restaurants and left without paying. It was a monotonous life, and by Friday night, Laboucan was hungry for more.

"I want to have sex with somebody," Laboucan told Bird and Briscoe. "Can you drive me around?"

The three climbed into Briscoe's rusted Ford Tempo and drove to 118th Avenue, where many of Edmonton's prostitutes lingered at street corners and bus stops. Briscoe drove with Bird beside him while Laboucan studied women they passed through the back windows. Eventually, they picked up a random woman in an alley, drove outside the city limits, and parked in a farmer's field.

Bird and Briscoe smoked cigarettes and waited in the dark outside the car while Laboucan had sex in the back seat. The couple's relationship was rocky. Briscoe didn't like driving Bird and her young friends around the city whenever they felt like it. At seventeen, Bird was more than a decade younger than her tall, meek boyfriend. Briscoe hated the way Laboucan openly flirted with Bird as though he wasn't there. It didn't help that Laboucan was her ex-boyfriend. There was no way Briscoe would leave them alone together, even if that meant being their chauffeur.

Laboucan finished and they drove the woman back into Edmonton and dropped her off on 118th Avenue.

"I want to have sex again," Laboucan said as soon as she left the car.

They picked up another woman waiting on the sidewalk, this one in a Denver Broncos T-shirt and sweatpants. At thirty-three, Ellie May Meyer was a kind, smart woman who knew the streets of Edmonton well. She still kept in touch with her family in British Columbia after more than a decade in Edmonton. She'd arrived in the city after drug problems and a criminal record derailed her plans to become a nurse and care for the elderly. Though Meyer rarely returned home, she never forgot to call her parents on birthdays and anniversaries. She had lived with a boyfriend for several months, but still worked 118th Avenue when she needed money.

Meyer sat with Laboucan in the back seat while Briscoe drove west on Yellowhead Trail. He parked in a different farmer's field and turned off the headlights. Again, he waited with Bird outside the car, the ground still rough and muddy with the remains of winter.

Suddenly, Meyer was out of the car and running past them, stumbling and desperate as she sprinted across the dark field. She kept moving even as both her shoes flew off and bounced away. Laboucan chased her. He tackled Meyer and they both tumbled to the ground. He pinned her down and beat her viciously.

When it was done, Laboucan walked back to the car with blood dripping from his hands.

Bird slowly approached Meyer's side and knelt down next to her. Her breath came out in rough, wet gurgles and her face was stained red. Through the fog of her injuries, Meyer tried to find a way to survive.

"I won't tell anyone," she whispered to Bird. "I'll go to the highway and find a ride. I'll tell people I fell."

Laboucan and Briscoe stared down at the dying Meyer. They told Bird to wait in the car. She obeyed.

There would be no mercy for Ellie May Meyer. Laboucan grabbed her left hand and cut off her pinky finger as a souvenir. She was still breathing when they abandoned the field where her body was found five weeks later.

The three drove back to Edmonton and returned to the Windmill Motel for the night.

Laboucan wrapped Meyer's severed finger in a bread bag and stashed it in the mini-fridge next to his hot dogs.

The next morning they woke late and headed to a nearby Humpty's Restaurant for breakfast. They skipped out on the bill after finishing their meal.

The three of them spent Saturday afternoon driving aimlessly around west Edmonton with no place to go. The previous night had done little to satiate Laboucan's appetite for violence.

"I want to kill someone," he said. "We're going to cut people's heads off and throw them in the street."

Briscoe was silent most of the day, still seething over his role as the driver and paranoid about Laboucan's interest in Bird.

Inevitably, they ended up at West Edmonton Mall. At the Circuit Circus arcade, a popular teen hangout, they met thirteen-year-old Nina Courtepatte and one of her friends. Both of them knew Snowman from the mall. He had a particular interest in Nina, whom he called Baby Girl.

Come with us, he told the girls. We're going to a bush party outside the city.

A fellow mall rat named Michael Williams and his young girlfriend joined them.

All seven of them were packed into Briscoe's Ford Tempo when they left the West Edmonton Mall parking lot that night. Nina sat on Laboucan's lap in the back seat as the group drove west out of Edmonton. There was excited talk of the party, and it was loud in the small car.

Behind the wheel, Briscoe was fed up with the younger crowd.

"Shut up," he told them repeatedly. No one listened. He was just the driver.

Outside the city, Briscoe turned off a secondary road and drove down a gravel lane until they reached a private strip blocked by a fence near the Edmonton Springs Golf Course. Briscoe stayed in the car studying a road map as the young people piled out and scattered.

The group eventually reached the fourth fairway of the golf course as the frosted grass crunched beneath their feet and their breath plumed in the cold air.

Laboucan rambled about killing people and bringing them back to life. He could barely stand still.

I don't think there's a bush party here, Nina whispered to her friend. They were uneasy, realizing they'd been lured into isolation.

Briscoe caught up to the group. He stood off to the side and said nothing as the teenagers milled about. They surrounded Nina and her friend like a gang of predators.

Bird turned on the girl first.

"You're pissing me off," she told Nina before she slid a wrench from her sleeve and swung it into the girl's back.

Nina fell to the ground, crying. "What did I do?"

She struggled to her feet, but Laboucan and Williams threw her back down to the ground. She pleaded desperately with the men who'd pretended to be her friends as they raped her. At one point, Briscoe held her down. The men beat her with a sledgehammer, a knife, and the wrench–anything they found in Briscoe's trunk to use as a weapon.

In the midst of the murder, Bird took Nina's horrified friend back to the car.

"You don't need to see this," Bird said.

In the morning, a golf course maintenance worker found the girl's body. That day, RCMP officers combed the fairway for evidence. They erected a tent to preserve the scene amidst wet flurries of snow.

A few days later, police caught their first break in the case. Williams' young girlfriend was caught shoplifting at West Edmonton Mall. She told security officers she was stealing hair dye because she'd witnessed a murder and wanted to change her appearance. She spotted Laboucan in the mall and pointed him out to security.

Within days, everyone involved named names and blamed each other for what had happened to Nina Courtepatte. Laboucan made no attempt to flee. Officers arrested him in a room he'd rented at the Fantasyland Hotel inside West Edmonton Mall.

All five of those who lured Nina and her friend to the golf course were convicted following seven years of investigation, trials, appeals, and conflicting testimony. Both Bird and Laboucan claimed Briscoe helped beat Ellie May Meyer, but neither were credible after years of lying about the case.

All of them acknowledged Laboucan as the ringleader. No one would have died if not for his violent sexual needs.

Laboucan was convicted of Nina's murder in March 2007. Police took a sample of his DNA, which linked him to Meyer's murder. In September 2011, Laboucan was on trial again to face those charges. Officers led him into the courtroom in chains. Though his lawyer did not challenge any of the prosecutor's evidence, he still refused to plead guilty. He was convicted in less than two hours.

Laboucan scowled at the floor through the proceedings. With family members of both his victims watching, he refused to say anything to the court.

Court of Queen's Bench Justice Sterling Sanderman called the removal of Meyer's finger a "grotesque act," as he stared at Laboucan in the prisoner's box.

"Why else would someone do that unless he was proud of what he had done?"

LEMON AND GOLD

Frank Lemon paced all night beside the embers of his campfire in the wilds of the Rocky Mountains. Close by, his friend and fellow prospector, Blackjack, was dead on his bedroll with a gruesome, gaping axe wound in his head. There was blood on Lemon's clothes. His best day had now been followed by his worst night. Only hours before, the two men believed they'd struck it rich.

In 1870, the prospectors had headed north from Tobacco Plains, Montana, to try their luck in the wild. Thirty-five years before Alberta became a province, the Crowsnest Pass in the Rocky Mountains was largely unexplored and veined with rumours of gold. It was still two decades before the Klondike rush would send thousands of prospectors north. Gold seekers were still trying to find the prime mining spots.

Originally, the two Americans planned to pan the banks of the North Saskatchewan River, but drifted west into the Rockies and hired two Stoney Indians to guide them into unfamiliar territory. Near the Highwood River, in the Livingstone Range, Lemon and Blackjack stumbled upon sparkles in a stream and followed the trail to a ledge thick with gold. The nearly pure samples were streaked with only thin lines of rock. As their guides watched, the prospectors celebrated their find along the isolated stream.

Their joy quickly soured into anger. The two fought over whether to depart immediately for the United States and return to their discovery better equipped, or simply camp where they were until the days warmed enough for easier travel.

Fuelled by greed, the men argued into the night until they tired and lay down by the warmth of their fire. Only Blackjack fell asleep.

The Stoney guides fled into the dark forest after witnessing Lemon murder his partner. As the sun rose, the prospector was in full flight back to Montana. He didn't stop until he'd returned to his Tobacco Plains home. Reportedly driven insane by grief, he soon confessed the killing to a priest.

All the details of Lemon's story were suspect. He was the sole witness to Blackjack's death and seemed raving mad to everyone he spoke with. Still, those who heard his story leaned closer when he mentioned his massive gold strike.

No, Lemon told them, I no longer remember where it was. He led several expeditions back to the Livingstone Range, but never found the gold, his camp, or the remains of the friend he'd left dead on his bedroll. Eventually, Lemon moved to Texas, though his tale inspired a lust among treasure hunters that lasted decades.

Stoney Indian Chief Bearspaw swore Lemon's guides to secrecy when he heard the story of Blackjack's murder. The chief feared any discovery of gold would only lead to hordes of greedy men stomping across fine hunting grounds. The chief's son eventually defied his father and led an expedition to find the gold years after Blackjack's killing. Later, the chief's grandson King continued the search, but could never get his grandfather to help him.

"He had no use for gold," King Bearspaw said about his grandfather. At the time, in 1958, King's search for the Lemon mine had lasted fifty years.

"I've had it in my blood since I was a boy," he told a *Calgary Herald* reporter. "It's been a dream to me all my life and I guess I'd sooner look for the lost Lemon Mine than do anything else. It's there. Somewhere."

Bearspaw hauled many sacks of rock from the claims he staked in the Livingstone Range. None of them held the gold he longed for. He renounced all his treaty rights to be unencumbered by rules about where he could live, hunt, and search for the mine. In between searches, Bearspaw hunted and trapped wildlife that wandered onto local ranches. Other treasure hunters sought him out as the acknowledged expert on the supposed mine. Their luck was no better than his.

Bearspaw's grandmother was always superstitious about the mine and warned him away from his lifelong obsession. A desire for riches would only drag him into unhappiness and death, she told him.

"I don't think the gold would have done me any harm," he said, "if I'd found it."

But he never did.

Others followed in his footsteps. The story of the lost Lemon mine passed down from counsellors to campers and grandparents to their grandchildren. Hopeful prospectors launched dozens of expeditions over the years, led by men certain they knew where to find the gold. Their guesses were wrong, their confidence unwarranted, and the maps in their hands complete fakes.

In the winter of 1931, nearly one hundred men scrambled into the Livingstone Range after rumours arose of the mine's second discovery.

Twenty-one-year-old Allie Streeter watched his father begin preparations immediately.

"A couple of guys figured they found colour," Streeter remembered. "They didn't keep their damn mouth shut."

The elder Streeter jumped in his pickup and drove directly from their Nanton-area ranch to Calgary. He returned hours later with a mining permit clutched in his hand. The father and son strapped supplies to a pair of ranch horses and set off on the twelve-hour journey west to the area called Flattop Mountain.

Amateur and professional prospectors made the same trip, clamouring across the prairie during a mild February. Though it was still early in the Great Depression, fathers and husbands were desperate for any chance at wealth. They weren't alone. All sorts of oddballs showed up. Streeter saw one man who stumbled through the woods in fancy Oxford shoes. He carried a large jug of wine instead of mining equipment.

"I didn't go as crazy as some of them," Streeter said. "They were out of their tree."

The rumour-inspired gold rush barely lasted a week.

Many desperate men staked claims with cornerstones and carved posts, but few dug into the ground. There weren't any disputes once the men realized there wasn't any gold.

As a senior, Streeter recalled his failed search fondly. "Supposing we had just laughed it off and stayed home and someone struck gold, wouldn't we have been a smart bunch of bastards?"

THE WORLD VERSUS
PATRICK CLAYTON

Patrick Clayton should have stuck out in the crowd of business suits and briefcases that filled the morning rush hour on 107th Street in downtown Edmonton. Only blocks from the sandstone dome of the provincial legislature and surrounded by government office buildings, the crowded stretch of sidewalk was full of workers as they stepped off buses and sipped from takeout coffee cups. Wider and taller than most people, Clayton wore a scowl on his weathered face and a battered brown jacket as he strode down the sidewalk with a backpack slung over one shoulder and a rifle case in his hand. Still, nobody paid him any attention, which he expected. None of them cared about him. No one did. He walked with a slump in front of several security cameras and hundreds of office windows, not caring that he might attract suspicion. Clayton stopped in front of the glass doors of the Workers' Compensation Board building, an eight-storey, block-long square of concrete that was the source of Clayton's rage.

The thirty-eight-year-old placed the rifle case on a sidewalk bench and took out his Browning bolt-action rifle. His backpack was heavy with enough ammunition to make a last stand and force Edmonton to notice him. They might even feel sorry for him if they heard what he had to say, he thought.

At 8:30 a.m. on October 21, 2009, Clayton barged through the glass doors and pointed his rifle at the first person he saw. Nadir Gova was two hours into his shift at the main security desk. He was accustomed to seeing protestors across the street with signs and stories of being cheated by the Workers' Compensation Board. Some weeks, they were out there every day yelling slogans at passing traffic and pedestrians. No one had ever come inside with a weapon before. Gova didn't even carry a gun.

"Lock this place down," Clayton yelled at him.

"Please don't shoot," Gova said. He raised his hands. "Just take it easy, buddy."

Gova moved back from his desk with a weave in his step. If this guy began to fire, he figured, a moving target would be harder to hit. Clayton mimicked each movement with the long barrel. There was little room to move behind the security desk, and Gova had to roll his chair away after he nearly fell over it. The security guard crouched behind the desk in a quick, desperate movement. He might be able to reach the alarm button under the desk if he wasn't shot before he could. It was pointless to lock down the building now that this furious man was already inside with the hundreds of employees already at work.

Without a detailed plan or much focus, Clayton became distracted as soon as Gova fell out of sight. To his left, women kept screaming when they saw the rifle he held at shoulder height. Clayton marched into the long room that opened off the lobby. Five terrified employees stared at him from behind the customer service counter. They'd all fallen silent.

"Girls," Clayton yelled at them. He pointed his rifle barrel to the tiled ceiling. "I want you to come over here right now."

The women ignored his order and dropped to the floor. Face down, they crawled away from the counter and into the cubicles beyond.

Gova saw his chance. He bolted from the cover of his desk and grabbed his security card in a desperate rush. The guard swiped his card at the security door panel behind his desk. A small bulb on the panel flashed green and the door opened. Gova paused only two steps from safety, remembering the alarm. He dove back to the security desk and hit the button that alerted police.

From the corner of his eye, Clayton saw Gova run through the open security door. Clayton forgot the women and stormed back to the security desk. He aimed the rifle.

Gova ran. Twenty feet behind him, Clayton fired a wayward shot as the guard sprinted through the elevator lobby. He escaped outside through the courier's entrance as a bullet tore into the wall behind him.

Clayton gave up on Gova and stood between the lobby and the elevators as the smell of burnt gunpowder began to spread.

Around the corner, Randy Morrow had waited for his doctor's appointment for half an hour by the time Clayton stormed the building. A WCB employee told him to arrive early and then they stuck him in a chair near the customer service area. He checked his watch. Typical. His injured shoulder was uncomfortable, and the appointment he'd come all the way from Peace River to attend was supposed to have started already.

Morrow no longer cared about any of that as he crouched behind the customer service desk and listened to the screams and the gunshot.

"Let's go."

Morrow looked up. Clayton towered over him. Morrow stood and raised his hands in the air. He didn't know what else to do.

"Do you have a cigarette?" Clayton asked. He hadn't thought to bring enough for what he had planned.

"Heck yes, I've got a cigarette." Morrow gave him a smoke and a lighter.

Clayton lit up and returned the lighter. "Thanks."

Receptionist Charlene Brown was on her way to the main floor to meet Morrow in the lobby. She knew Morrow's doctor wasn't even in the building yet, but the guy could at least wait upstairs since he'd showed up early. She heard a bang just as she entered the stairwell. Likely a problem with the elevators, she thought.

Brown saw smoke as she stepped out of the stairwell, but the fire alarm was silent. It smelled like a cigarette. She walked to the security desk and found it empty. The lobby was deserted. Perhaps the women in customer service knew what was going on.

When Brown turned the corner, only Morrow and Clayton were there, and the lit cigarette was still between the gunman's fingers. He pointed the rifle at her with his other hand.

"Open the door."

Brown led them to the security door Gova had escaped through and swiped her card.

Shaun Donnelly walked out of the elevator and nearly bumped into Clayton. The case manager from the eighth floor was wearing his parka and planned to go outside for a smoke of his own. With the rifle, Clayton gestured at him to turn around.

He herded his three hostages into an elevator car. He wanted the top floor, he told them, and they would need a big room with a table and chairs once they got there. The doors opened and a maintenance man waiting to go down gave the group a confused smile. On the eighth floor, no one knew anything was wrong.

Clayton jabbed the rifle barrel into his chest. "This is not a joke."

Clayton randomly collected hostages as he went. Anyone he happened to pass in the cubicles and halls was forced to walk in front of him until there was a parade of people headed to the main conference room. Some workers were unaware anything was wrong as they checked their morning emails and discussed the previous night's television shows.

"You have to come with me," he told them as he smoked and smirked. For once, Clayton was in control of everyone he met. Now, people were finally paying attention to him. Clayton herded Morrow into the conference room with eight of the WCB employees he believed had helped ruin him.

Clayton locked the door. "Make yourselves comfortable because we are going to be here for a while."

Beside the flip charts and plants that lined the walls, the hostages sat as far from the gunman as possible. Clayton emptied his backpack on the table in front of the crying group. Several boxes of ammunition, a plastic baggie holding more bullets, balls of yellow twine, and a knife spilled out.

He tossed the twine to his captives and ordered them to tie their hands in front of them. Most of the hostages tied themselves as loosely as they dared, and Clayton never bothered to check. He told one of them to draw the blinds because he thought police would soon have a sniper on the buildings across the street.

Clayton wanted to play a CD of songs he'd created for his hostages, but the computer on the table wouldn't load the music. Instead, the room was filled with sharp breaths and sobs. Several of the hostages believed they wouldn't leave the room alive.

A hostage called 911 on the conference room phone, and Clayton pressed the speaker button so everyone could listen. He told the dispatcher his name and admitted he'd taken people captive. He wanted to talk to the chief of police.

Some of the hostages were now worried more about Donnelly than themselves. Obviously ill, the case manager had a red face, and his rasping breaths were louder than anyone's sobs. I have high blood pressure, he told the others. You should leave, Clayton said to him. First, all the hostages wrote their names in a notebook for Donnelly to take to police.

Clayton recounted his tale of woe as the notebook was passed around. While on a carpentry job in 2002, he'd ripped up his knee when he tripped over some rebar at a work site. He'd hurt the same knee several times before, he said, but this was the worst. A year later, a WCB doctor aggravated the injury during a post-surgery examination. Clayton was given a second corrective surgery, but all that did was force him into a painkiller addiction, he complained to his hostages. When the WCB cut off his medication benefits for lying to them about a secret job he'd taken, what other choice did he have but to turn to a crack cocaine addiction? When the WCB gave him $11,000 in benefits, it was their fault he'd spent it all on a month's worth of drugs.

He just wanted to be heard, Clayton repeatedly told his captives. He would apologize to them one minute and turn furious the next. He cried while he talked about how long it had been since he'd seen his estranged son.

"This is my last stand," he told them. "I'm not leaving here. I'm not going to jail. Too late for me. I'm done."

Donnelly expected a bullet in the back when he left the room with the list of names less than forty-five minutes after Clayton arrived. Outside, he was greeted by yellow police tape and tactical officers who questioned him about what he'd seen. A whole section of Edmonton's downtown was cordoned off.

Clayton repeatedly hung up on police negotiators if they didn't say what he wanted to hear. At times, he only wanted to speak with reporters and called the local CBC station on a hostage's cellphone. He forced his captives to type out his story and send it to various television stations.

Clayton angrily refused when negotiators asked him to let more people walk out unharmed.

However, when hostages asked to go to the washroom unescorted, Clayton was ambivalent about the fact police would grab them and escort them from the building.

"I know you will probably not come back and I don't fucking care," he told one of his captives.

Clayton told police he'd released a number of hostages in good faith. He promised the remaining hostages he wouldn't hurt them and then minutes later, over the phone, promised negotiators he would. A police robot delivered the food and water he demanded. Two WCB employees were traded for more cigarettes as the afternoon wore on. Clayton let hostages walk out the door one after another during the first six hours of the standoff. At times, he didn't seem interested in keeping any of them.

By late afternoon, the only two that remained in the conference room were Clayton and Morrow, the sole hostage not employed by the WCB. The two men shared a frustration about their troubled experiences with the WCB. Morrow empathized with Clayton's woes, though not his violent response. As they bonded, Morrow believed the two might both survive the day.

Eventually, Clayton put the rifle down.

"I'll walk out with you," Morrow offered.

Clayton shook his head, took a bullet from the plastic baggie, and gave it to Morrow as a memento. Then he let his last hostage walk out to the corridor where police waited.

Shortly after 6:00 p.m., Clayton heard the police order him out of the conference room. He left his rifle behind and was pinned to the floor by officers.

During the ten-hour ordeal, only one shot was fired, and no one was hurt.

Though Clayton offered his victims a brief apology at his trial, he remained defiant and saved his most heartfelt words for a long speech about those who had wronged him.

"I am a political prisoner of a corporate bully," he read from a crumpled piece of paper. "During this WCB claim I have suffered significant psychological, physical and emotional despair that has dehumanized me in every way possible."

Clayton was sentenced to eleven years in prison.

GARRY BARRETT'S
BITTER GRUDGE

From the day he arrived at the Alberta Penitentiary in 1908, Garry Barrett held a secret grudge against Richard Stedman, the prison's deputy warden. From the very beginning, Barrett regularly railed to Stedman about the unjust murder trial that led to his life sentence for shooting his ten-year-old stepson.

The boy had jumped in front of his mother during a violent fight in the family home near Prince Albert, Saskatchewan. Barrett's death sentence was commuted to life because a doctor botched his treatment of the child's gunshot wound.

"It was me that done it but it was an accident," Barrett told people about the boy's death. "It was a self-cocker and it went off."

Barrett became angry when Stedman could do nothing to help, and the relationship between them soured further when Stedman refused to allow Barrett the repeated doctor's visits he requested for minor ailments. It seemed a small thing, but it festered inside him until the morning of March 15 the following year, when Barrett calmly stood up from his workbench in the prison's machine shop and slammed a hatchet into Richard Stedman's skull.

Even inside the Edmonton prison's walls, the murder shocked the four inmates who witnessed it. They regarded Barrett, a small man, morose and withdrawn, as far more bitter than dangerous. Stedman had been an authority and was therefore not universally liked by the inmates, though none of the others disliked him enough to kill him.

Barrett had scowled at Stedman ten minutes before the murder, but the other inmates hadn't cared. Barrett was never in a good mood and scowled all the time. He'd complained loudly that he hadn't slept the night before. The five other men in the prison's machine shop didn't even have time to yell a warning before Barrett nearly took Richard Stedman's head off from behind. Stedman was leaning over another bench with the prison's carpentry instructor. He fell to the floor bloodied, and died in the prison's medical wing less than an hour later.

The fifty-seven-year-old Barrett stood still after his violent chop at Stedman. He handed the stained weapon to the carpentry instructor and quietly waited for the guards to come. His calm demeanour was disturbing. Once the guards put him back in his cell, two of them stood watch so Barrett didn't kill himself. The warden came to Barrett's guarded cell to ask why he'd killed Stedman.

"I would not have done it," Barrett told him, "if the deputy had let me see the doctor."

Barrett had only been in Canada a few years before going to prison. He was born in Detroit, married young, and had eight children in quick succession. He took them all to Chicago. Eventually, he left that family and married a Mormon woman in Utah. Barrett would end up shooting her son once they moved north.

A coroner's jury took less than a day to conclude its investigation into Stedman's death. With witnesses and a confession, it wasn't difficult. Barrett was charged with murder. A six-man jury was assembled for a trial two days later.

Barrett pleaded not guilty by reason of insanity. A doctor testified that Barrett's lack of sleep, his feeling sick, and his constant brooding could produce an unsound mind. Surely, the doctor said, a sane man wouldn't have done this.

Barrett testified that Stedman never liked him and often gave him dirty looks. Barrett claimed he'd once called him "a dirty cur." Stedman sneered at him the morning he died, the convict said.

Although he said he'd forgotten details, Barrett repeated his confession.

"I struck him, but I don't know how I hit him or where."

The jury took five minutes to convict him.

"Garry Barrett, stand up," Judge Horace Harvey said. "Have you anything to say why sentence should not be passed upon you?"

Barrett lifted his head and stood. His voice trembled. "I have been imposed upon all my life. My life was threatened."

Harvey sentenced him to hang in the Alberta Penitentiary yard on July 14, 1909.

Barrett sat back down.

The morning of his execution, before sunrise, Barrett ate his last breakfast and smoked his last pipe in his cell before they came for him.

"Are you ready?" a guard asked him.

"Yes."

The rope was tightened around his neck, then loosened to give him breath enough for his last words.

"I would like to state just how it happened. Gentlemen, I am going to be hanged, but I killed the deputy warden in self-defence. Had I not done so, my flesh would not be the food for vultures."

His strangulation was not quick. It took fifteen minutes for Barrett to die.

The anonymous, masked executioner wore the same boots issued to all guards at the Alberta Penitentiary. Later, he sliced the rope that hanged Barrett into pieces and distributed them to prison staff.

PARANOID

Martin Charles Ostopovich lost his mind during the last five years of his life.

The forty-one-year-old hadn't been the same since his truck rolled off a Yukon highway in 1999. Martin was lucky to be alive, but he suffered severe head injuries and needed extensive surgery to close his wounds. It was weeks before he left the hospital. When he returned home, Martin was still the same father of two, an avid outdoorsman who took his wife, Wendy, camping and fixed other people's cars in his spare time.

Still, Wendy remembered the doctors' warnings while her husband was unconscious. A head injury could come back to haunt him in a year or more, one of them said.

Three years later, Martin told his wife the local radio stations were talking about him. Inside the Ostopovich home on a cul-de-sac in Spruce Grove, a suburban community just west of Edmonton, he grew increasingly paranoid. On one particularly bad day, he dug into his neck with a blade because he believed RCMP officers had implanted a transmitter under his skin. Everyone was suddenly against him.

Wendy went to doctors alone after her husband refused to see them. A psychiatrist told her he couldn't treat an unwilling patient unless they became a direct threat to someone's safety. Desperate for help, Wendy walked through the front door of the Spruce Grove RCMP detachment in the spring of 2002. She told them about her husband's head injury and the dangerous, unstable person he'd become. He has guns, she added.

Officers apprehended Martin and involuntarily committed him to the Royal Alexandra Hospital for two weeks.

In hospital, it didn't take long for doctors to diagnose him as a paranoid schizophrenic. To placate him, they performed a CAT scan of Martin's head to prove there was no tracking device implanted inside him. At the end of the two-week committal, he accepted a prescription and walked out of the Royal Alexandra against doctors' advice. Wendy and the RCMP officers could only watch helplessly. Wendy was shocked her husband was allowed to leave treatment at all, but the hospital could only hold an involuntary patient who hadn't broken any laws for so long. Doctors wanted to ration his medication so he'd have to visit the hospital to receive his doses, but weren't allowed to. There would be no support.

Martin called his devoted wife a "commie" for helping police force him into a hospital bed. This word was his shorthand for anyone he believed was plotting against him. He soon went to court in an effort to recover the guns police had seized from him. His application was denied.

For months, Martin took his pills and seemed calmer under their influence. Then he cut back to taking them every other day. When he stopped altogether, Wendy moved out for a month and only came back because he agreed to start taking the medication once more. Later, he stopped again.

He spent more and more time at home alone. It was hard for Martin to hold down a job when he told co-workers about the voices in his head and "the pinkos" who conspired against him. By February 2004, he was worse than he'd ever been, and had acquired more guns.

On the night of February 27, Wendy came home to their pale-yellow bungalow to find loud music blaring on the stereo and her husband at the kitchen table with a near-empty bottle of rye in his hand. She knew he rarely drank so much. She turned around and immediately left the house.

"I don't even think he realized I was there," she would later say.

Wendy spent the cold night in her car outside of a hockey arena and came home at sunrise to an angry husband mumbling about "commies" in his home.

Outside, a neighbour discovered a bullet hole in the door of their car, which faced the Ostopovich home. The two Spruce Grove officers who responded to the 911 call remembered how they'd committed Martin to hospital two years before. They knew he'd react badly to officers at his door.

Frantic, Wendy came outside and told the officers they couldn't go inside. When he saw the police, Martin went to his bedroom, where he kept two high-powered rifles.

The officers retreated and took Wendy with them. Over their radios, they told the detachment to send backup. By the time Martin called a local news station and promised "someone is going to die today," officers had blocked off traffic and told neighbours to stay in their basements.

Martin was still on the phone in his kitchen as police surrounded the house. He called and ranted at two television stations before he hung up. Next, he made a livid phone call to the RCMP. He called the officer who answered a "fucking rat" and declared the next person to pass his house would get shot.

Martin told the officer he knew the RCMP had installed a camera in his eye. He wanted them to let him see Wendy one more time. At one point, he screamed so loudly officers could hear him a block away.

The local police had heard enough and called the heavily armed Emergency Response Team in Edmonton. They fixed his phone line so he could only reach police.

The cavalry arrived just after 4:00 p.m., and white-clad snipers were soon climbing onto the roofs of surrounding homes. Next-door neighbour Casey Van Leeuwen watched in shock as one officer crawled through his daughter's bedroom window, seeking a better view of the neighbourhood from the home's wide living room window.

"It was really bizarre," he said. "It was like a movie."

The tactical team recognized the beginnings of a bad situation. Martin could see the whole cul-de-sac because his house was nestled deep between two others. Officers were forced to hide behind neighbouring homes and rely on the snipers as their eyes. An hour later, Martin went outside to get a CD from his truck's glove compartment, and the closest officers didn't realize it until he was back inside.

Constable David Wilkinson wasn't having any better luck on the phone, parked blocks away at the mobile command centre. Martin talked a lot about dying in a police shootout.

"I'm going to take it to you," he told Wilkinson, and repeated only one demand throughout his rants. Above all else, he wanted to say goodbye to his wife.

As long as Martin was alone and the street was clear, he wasn't a danger to others, police reasoned, but his truck was parked directly outside the side door. He could be behind the wheel in seconds. Police couldn't block the vehicle or disable it with gunshots. Martin would realize there was a full tactical team outside. Officers began planning their strategy should he make a run for it.

Wilkinson counted the minutes on the clock. He assumed Martin would watch the evening news at six o'clock to see if his phone calls were reported. Then, he would learn from the media gathered near the command centre that heavily armed officers were outside. It would destroy any trust Wilkinson had managed to build. Wilkinson thought he'd made some progress. Martin had discussed music with him for several minutes before retrieving the CD from his truck.

Wilkinson hoped telling Martin he was outgunned would get him to surrender. Instead, it infuriated him. Slamming the phone down, he grabbed both his rifles by the barrels and headed outside to his truck.

An RCMP SUV slid around the icy corner and sped into the cul-de-sac. Corporal Jim Galloway, a thirty-year veteran of the Mounties and a dog handler, was behind the wheel. The fifty-three-year-old Galloway had insisted on driving. He wanted to be in the middle of the plan, and it was hard to refuse his experience and skill. Galloway told his family he wasn't ever the first guy through the door, that others were in greater danger, but his fellow officers knew that wasn't always true.

Constable Tim Taniguchi sat in the passenger's seat. He and Galloway knew the plan. They would ram Martin's vehicle with their own, then rush outside and take cover. Martin would be jostled and shocked long enough for other officers to arrest him. His truck might even roll onto its side and knock him unconscious, officers thought.

It was a sound, if desperate, plan. Constable Randy Pearson, who led the emergency team, knew it was dangerous.

"I was comfortable as you can be with ramming a vehicle with an armed man inside," he would later say. "How comfortable can anyone be with that?"

Galloway stamped on the SUV's accelerator as Martin backed his pickup down the driveway. For a moment, Taniguchi and Martin looked directly at each other through the windows, and then there was a scream of metal and impact.

Broadsided, Martin's truck slid sideways on the ice and wedged against his neighbours' cars parked in the half-circle of street. The impact barely registered. He never even lost his grip on the steering wheel.

Galloway slammed the RCMP vehicle into park, and both men yanked on the door handles. Through his open window, Martin pointed one of his rifles at Taniguchi through the SUV's windshield. The officer ducked to the floor and hoped the shots couldn't penetrate the engine block.

Still seated in his truck, Martin turned his rifle and fired a fatal shot into Galloway as he stepped out of the SUV.

Other officers in full sprint fired a barrage of shots into the cab of the truck that shattered the remaining glass. Martin Ostopovich died instantly, only twenty seconds after he had hung up on Wilkinson.

The next day, Martin's mother-in-law, Shirley Eldon, said he'd fallen victim to his own mind before any police bullet.

"I just don't want people to think Marty was a monster. We want people to understand more about this illness so it doesn't happen again. It didn't need to happen. The voices took over."

ART OF THE DEAL

In April 1982, Peter Pocklington lived the sweet life.
Years before he became a pariah in Edmonton, the man known as Peter Puck was the city's wealthiest success story. Everything he touched turned to gold. He owned a meat-packing plant, car dealerships, real estate, and stakes in investment firms. Men that rich didn't make their tax returns public, but Pocklington was thought to be worth more than $100 million. The bearded smiler was friends with actor Paul Newman and former United States President Gerald Ford. His office occupied the penthouse in one of downtown Edmonton's tallest buildings. A Porsche and a Rolls Royce were parked in his garage.

Pocklington dominated the local sports market. He owned the Drillers of the National Professional Soccer League and the Trappers baseball team of the Pacific Coast League. Most importantly, the forty-year-old owned the Edmonton Oilers, the orange and blue blood running through the city's veins. Pocklington bought into the Oilers when they were a World Hockey Association team in 1976. Two years later, he acquired the rights to a promising young rookie, Wayne Gretzky. The team was on the verge of a dynasty that would last nearly a decade.

"I thought I was bulletproof," Pocklington later told his biographers, "until I was shot."

On the morning of April 20, Pocklington was getting into his Rolls Royce when a masked gunman pointed a loaded .357 magnum at his head. It was a huge gun, the kind that led to closed caskets at funerals. Pocklington went cold. It looked like a cannon.

"Do as I tell you or I'm going to kill you."

Pocklington led the man in the black balaclava from the garage inside his seven-bedroom mansion near the North Saskatchewan River Valley. Eva Pocklington was on the phone in the kitchen when her husband walked in with a gun to his head. She screamed and hung up with a slam.

The man with the gun asked who else was in the house. Housekeeper Carmen Mitchell and babysitter Joseph Wright were in the living room, though Pocklington's young son was at school. The intruder placed a spool of wire and a knife on the kitchen table. He forced Wright to tie Mitchell and Pocklington to chairs in the living room. Eva tied Wright, and she was left free.

The masked man said he was there to abduct Eva for $2 million.

Pocklington, always the businessman, began to negotiate. Two million on short notice was a lot of money, even for one of Edmonton's richest men.

In a small voice, Eva asked the gunman if he'd like a cup of coffee.

"Eva, be quiet," Pocklington said. "We're doing a deal here."

Less than an hour after he arrived, the masked man settled on a ransom of $1 million.

Nearby, the neighbour Eva was on the phone with called Pocklington's office. The scream and sudden hang-up made her suspicious. Pocklington's secretary called the home. Eva picked up and, thinking quickly, called the secretary by the wrong name and said she couldn't make an appointment they didn't have. That was enough for the secretary to call 911 and report that something wasn't right in the Pocklington home.

Police converged on the central Edmonton neighbourhood, and reporters weren't far behind. The biggest show in Edmonton that day had begun.

Inside, the .357 Magnum was pointed at Eva. She would leave with him, the gunman said, and Pocklington would hand over the cash that night.

When Eva and her captor raised the garage door, a police officer was standing on the driveway. In bare feet and an "I Love New York" sweater, she bolted to the officer with tears in her eyes.

"Three of them are tied up in the living room," she said breathlessly.

"Peter tied them up?" the confused officer asked.

"Yes. No! The kidnapper."

"Which three?"

"My cleaning lady," Eva said. "My babysitter. Peter."

Eva thought police might grab the kidnapper before he went back in the house, but he'd already retreated. His threat to kill those inside if she tried to escape echoed in her head.

"Oh," she moaned. "I wonder if I've done the wrong thing."

Inside, beneath the balaclava, twenty-nine-year-old Mirko Petrovic was desperate. The Yugoslavian immigrant's plan was an hour old and already in shambles. His intended target was safe with the police that now surrounded the house. Panic rose in his chest.

Petrovic, a quiet man with a thick moustache and thicker eastern European accent, was nearly broke after six years in Canada. A concrete company he owned in Fort McMurray briefly prospered before it succumbed to poor sales and bad management. In northern Alberta's construction industry, Petrovic was known to carry pockets full of cash and give generous tips to drivers who delivered his concrete to work sites.

His business sunk, Petrovic moved to Edmonton and remained unemployed for months as he tried to support himself and his girlfriend. Petrovic feared bankruptcy and mulled endlessly over his financial mire. He worried when he was a day late on his rent, his landlady said.

Petrovic was strung out when he came back inside and moved Pocklington to a room on the third floor. The employees stayed tied up on the ground floor.

Pocklington continued to sell. It was the deal of his life.

"This is the best thing that's ever happened to you," he said to his captor.

Pocklington told the masked Petrovic about D. B. Cooper, a legendary American airplane hijacker who had pulled off a perfect crime. In 1972, Cooper forced a flight to land in Seattle when he brought what appeared to be a bomb on board. Cooper let the passengers leave and collected $200,000 in cash. He told the pilots that remained to fly him to Mexico. On the way, Cooper strapped the money to his chest and parachuted off the plane. He was never seen again. Got away clean. The Federal Bureau of Investigation assumed Cooper died a violent death in a failed skydive, but Pocklington didn't tell Petrovic that. The businessman was on a roll.

I even have my own plane, Pocklington added.

"That's how we'll play it," Petrovic replied after a few minutes of silence.

Later that morning, a police negotiator phoned the house for the first time. Petrovic held the phone to Pocklington's ear as he remained tied in the chair.

"I understand you have a problem," the officer said.

Pocklington said it was fine. "We are well on our way to getting this deal put together."

Pocklington told the negotiator what to do. He and Petrovic would need a clear path to the Edmonton City Centre Airport. Police should collect the million-dollar ransom as soon as possible, he said.

During those negotiations, police asked that Wright and Mitchell be released. Petrovic agreed and sent them out the front door. All he really needed now was the rich guy.

At police headquarters, Chief Robert Lunney was anxious. Pocklington was a difficult man to deal with on a good day, and now he had a gun to his head. The businessman was dictating his own kidnapping in a direction Lunney didn't want to go. Right now, the situation was contained to two men in one house. Pocklington wanted the gunman in the open, going through public streets to the airport. It was ridiculous, and it was dangerous.

Pocklington's neighbourhood was a circus. Hundreds of spectators, police officers, and reporters crowded as close to the house as investigators allowed. People all over Edmonton heard radio reports and hurried to Saskatchewan Drive, across the North Saskatchewan River from the provincial legislature on the opposite bank. Some brought lawn chairs and watched through binoculars. A sandwich cart was set up nearby.

"It's better than the movies and it's free," said one man who'd come from the suburb of St. Albert to watch.

Lunney couldn't let the gunman walk out to that madness. This debacle stayed inside the Pocklington home until it was finished, the chief decided. Lunney began to make his own arrangements.

Through the afternoon, Pocklington remained wired to a chair while Petrovic stood over him. The businessman lost patience with the police as the hours passed. The next time they called, he demanded to talk to Eva and tried to force the police to follow his instructions. They should be on their way to the airport already, he thought. Afterwards, an officer came on the line and said they were doing all they could.

"Yeah, sure," Pocklington said.

By early evening, Lunney had the $1 million in cash and his own plan. Unlike Pocklington, the chief wasn't so sure the gunman wouldn't start shooting. Petrovic told negotiators he didn't care if he lived or died. He mentioned shooting himself in the head. If the gunman truly had nothing to lose, Lunney believed they needed to end the situation quickly, and that didn't include a ride to the airport.

Lunney's main concern was the gunman's presence on the third floor. It would be difficult for officers to get upstairs without being heard. They needed to draw him to the ground floor, and Lunney had the suitcase full of one-hundred-dollar bills as bait.

The chief sent the ransom inside with four tactical officers. He ordered they leave the money in the kitchen and hide themselves on the ground floor. The officers snuck inside during a negotiation call, when any inadvertent noises would be covered by the conversation.

Lunney knew the gunman would be enraged when he discovered tactical officers in the home. They couldn't give him any time to do something stupid. They needed to be quick.

"I gave the order to shoot to kill," Lunney later told reporters.

Four officers left the money by the kitchen doorway, chose hiding spots, and waited.

More than three hours later, negotiators called Petrovic and said his cash was in the kitchen and his ride to the airport was ready. Pocklington, restrained at the wrists and ankles with wire, took small steps as he led Petrovic downstairs. The .357 Magnum was pressed into the millionaire's back.

In the kitchen, Petrovic immediately saw the cash. Pocklington stooped and struggled to pick up the heavy suitcase. As they were distracted, an officer with an M-16 rifle slid into the kitchen.

"Don't move! Police!"

Petrovic turned. The officer fired one shot that grazed Pocklington and nearly ripped off Petrovic's right arm below the elbow.

Moments later, Pocklington awoke on his kitchen floor bloodied from superficial wounds to his arm and chest.

He was safe. He was furious.

"Do you know who you just shot, assholes?"

Outside, spectators ran madly in all directions as the shot echoed through the neighbourhood. Some hurried away while others sprinted in for a closer look.

The next day, Pocklington allowed photographers and reporters into his room at the University of Alberta Hospital. A picture of the bandaged and grinning Pocklington landed on the *Edmonton Journal*'s front page. He stayed in hospital for three days. Eva brought him food from the outside because he hated what the hospital gave him.

At the other end of the hospital's emergency ward, Petrovic was handcuffed to his bed as three officers kept watch. He'd undergone major surgery to save his arm. It was in a cast when lawyers visited his bedside to charge him officially.

Petrovic pleaded guilty to kidnapping and was sentenced to fifteen years in prison. He was released after five and sent back to Yugoslavia.

A week after the ransom attempt, Lunney ate lunch with a displeased Pocklington.

"Everything in life is a deal," the millionaire told the chief. "You should have listened to me."

LIKE FATHER, LIKE SON

In the dim pre-dawn of the Fort Saskatchewan Jail, William McLean walked the dirty concrete floor to his father's cell in loose slippers. It was a frigid November day in 1933. The inmates along death row could see their breath. The twenty-year-old stopped to stare through the bars at Kenneth McLean's weathered face and the crooked nose of a man who liked to fight. The older man's body was dotted with bullet wounds and lined with knife slashes. When drunk, Kenneth liked to yank up his shirt and show off the scars to anyone in sight.

"Goodbye, father," William said.

The two had shared time in many jail cells over the past fourteen months, ever since they murdered a wheat farmer on his porch. The wandering father and son spent the previous summer as threshers on various farms in central Alberta that needed extra hands. William accompanied his sixty-year-old father from job to job, and most nights they drank their wages dry. The rough men would simply head to the next farm once they wore out their welcome. Sometimes they told employers their real names, and other times they concocted various false identities. In between farms, tired of manual labour under the hot sun, the two hatched a simple plan for quicker money.

On the night of September 30, 1932, the McLeans drove a stolen car to the farm of Walter Parsille, a former boss of theirs who lived alone near Mannville. Parsille's dog barked at the two men as they parked their car and walked up the driveway. Kenneth hid behind a shed in the front yard and shot Parsille when he strolled onto the porch to investigate the nighttime visitor. Kenneth let the empty rifle shell fall to the ground.

Parsille died in his doorway with a hole in his chest. Kenneth went through his pockets and stole more than $400. The plan started as a robbery, but the McLeans decided they couldn't rob a man they knew and let him live. Kenneth had rotted in prisons across Canada and the United States and hated the idea of a return trip.

The McLeans drove away and left Parsille where he lay. Neighbours found him when they came to investigate why his dog had been constantly barking for two days.

The father and son added another two days to their head start before RCMP officers identified the killers and began the hunt. The father and son fled southeast into Saskatchewan and made a brief stop at a relative's farm in Eastend before they darted south across the American border. Officers nearly caught them in St. Paul, Minnesota, where the pair stopped at a Northeast National Bank to exchange Parsille's money for American bills.

Kenneth and William continued south through Iowa and Missouri. They were headed for Tennessee, where Kenneth once lived and some of his relatives still did.

The two decided to run in different directions and split up after they crossed their final state line. The separation didn't last long. William was arrested within days after he stole a car in Knoxville.

Kenneth should never have returned to Tennessee. He'd fled as an escaped fugitive in 1915, ten months into a ten-year prison sentence for a Knoxville murder. He'd shot a man on the steps of a church on a Sunday morning. Kenneth was recognized and arrested in Chattanooga. He still carried the rifle that killed Parsille, and officers still held the shell he'd let fall to the ground.

Before his father joined him behind bars in Knoxville, William shared a cell with inmate Eugene Ward. William told him he'd thought of escaping.

"Why try and escape if you're not guilty?" Ward asked.

"Trouble is, I am," William said.

The Mounties met the McLeans at the Knoxville jail and brought them back to Alberta chained to one another. Each night, the father and son shared a holding cell in a different town.

They were tried separately at Vegreville's new courthouse in the summer of 1933. William was convicted on Ward's testimony, and Kenneth was found guilty after his son took the stand. The son testified that his father killed Parsille alone and William fought with him about the deed afterwards. He'd only stayed with his father out of family loyalty, William claimed. The court saw through the lies, and the lenient sentence William hoped for never materialized.

"I'm ready for the rap," a weary Kenneth told the court. "I've faced death too often to try and squeal out of it now."

Kenneth later tried to tell RCMP investigators his son actually hadn't been at the Parsille farm. It was a rare fatherly gesture no one believed.

As October began, the McLeans were only days away from the noose. In the death row cells of Fort Saskatchewan's jail, they could hear the hammering of nails as their gallows were built. The pair were scheduled to be the first executions at the new prison.

"Do you want a couple of good men to build the scaffold?" Kenneth called out from his cell window.

His offer of help was turned down.

From his cell, Kenneth stared through the iron bars at his son.

"Goodbye son. We've travelled many a rough trail together and we'll travel this one. We'll keep on going the same way."

Kenneth followed his son to the gallows twenty-two minutes later.

STRAY BULLET

Brazilian student Jose Neto was falling in love with Calgary on the night he was shot in the face while walking home after dinner with his girlfriend.

The twenty-five-year-old had studied international business and improved his broken English for eight months before the night of September 16, 2008. His girlfriend, Roberta Porto, had moved to his adopted city three months before. The young couple had met on a Brazilian beach before he left for Canada. Together, they'd travelled to Banff and Lake Louise and were awed by the Rocky Mountains. Previously, the pair had only seen the mountains on television. They eventually planned to move to Spain so Jose could learn Spanish, then return to Brazil. For now, they were happy at home in Calgary.

They'd eaten a late dinner in Chinatown Tuesday night and cut through the shadows of Circle Park during a leisurely walk to their inner-city home. Around 9:30, they stopped at a park bench to chat among the changing colours of the trees.

The couple didn't notice anyone else in the park. They concentrated only on each other until a sharp crack of sound echoed around them.

A bright flash of white filled Jose's world. For a moment, he thought he'd somehow been hit with a massive electrical shock. Everything went black. The park vanished. Roberta was gone. Jose panicked.

"What happened?" Jose desperately asked. "What happened?"

"I don't know," Roberta said. His face was bloody. She was horrified. "I don't know."

"Look at me," he begged her. He put his hands to his face. Both his eyes were torn apart. "What happened?"

"I think it was a shot," she said. She screamed for help.

"I think I'm going to die." He stumbled to the ground.

"No, you're talking to me."

"I'm going to be blind," Jose moaned.

Roberta screamed into the night. "Telephoner a policia!"

* * *

At thirty, Roland Warawa had spent nearly a third of his life behind bars. He'd been expelled from high school in the tenth grade. That same day, his mother told him he needed to get a job or find his own place. Warawa, never one for honest work, moved out. He'd done more work in prison programs than in any employment on the outside. At nineteen, he'd botched an armed robbery at a strip-mall jewelry store. He and a partner entered a vacant property in the mall and dropped into the jewelry store through the ceiling tiles the next morning. The robbery went smoothly until police officers pulled into the parking lot. Warawa panicked and shot the store owner in the neck.

The man collapsed to the floor and played dead.

"Oh shit," his partner said. "You've killed him. You've made it worse."

"I don't care," Warawa replied.

"Are you going to shoot the cops too?"

"I don't care," Warawa repeated.

As he fled the scene, Warawa fired wayward shots at two officers with a .22-calibre handgun before he was arrested in a nearby alley. He was sentenced to more than a decade in prison for attempted murder.

His 2004 statutory release lasted less than a year before he was sent back inside for parole violations. Months later, he assaulted a police officer who arrested him for shoplifting a T-shirt. Once released, he showed up high to a meeting with his parole officer. The last of his sentences expired in February 2008, and he was a free man on Calgary's streets.

Warawa avoided police attention for six months. Then, in September, he visited a friend of a friend and smoked crack cocaine for hours. When he arrived home, Robert Reitmeier was furious that his roommate had allowed the unknown Warawa to get high in their place.

"My home isn't a crack house," Reitmeier told Warawa.

Warawa pulled a revolver from his belt. From ten feet away, he coldly studied the man yelling at him.

"Are you going to shoot me?" Reitmeier asked. He pointed at his own forehead.

Warawa shot him in the belly.

Twelve days later, on the same night Jose and Roberta enjoyed a late dinner and a romantic walk, Warawa was in Circle Park with his girlfriend, Maureen MacGugan. It would still be three days before Reitmeier picked him out of a police lineup as the man who shot him. He was a wanted man with his revolver still stuck in his waistband.

In Circle Park, forty metres from where Jose and Roberta sat, Warawa and his girlfriend ran into a couple they knew, Michael Martel and Debra McLean. The couples chatted and the conversation turned to a possible cocaine deal. Warawa abruptly changed the subject and demanded Martel return a cellphone that belonged to MacGugan. The conversation quickly became angry among the four of them. They began to yell at each other.

MacGugan stepped forward and punched McLean in the face. "Don't speak to Roland that way."

In a moment, Martel struck MacGugan across the jaw and sent her to the ground bloody. "Don't touch my wife."

Warawa unzipped his pants as his girlfriend crumpled to the ground. He pulled his revolver from a sock stuffed in the crotch of his jeans.

Warawa brought the revolver up and fired at Martel.

He missed and the shot streaked across the park.

The two couples fled.

Two days later, Calgary police officers watched as Warawa left his house just after noon in his white Lexus. In just forty-eight hours, more than sixty Calgary police officers took part in the hunt for the man who shot Jose Neto. Officers watched as he made a short stop at a grocery store to use a pay phone. The most wanted man in Calgary then parked, walked a few blocks, and got into a taxi at a Best Western Hotel. Each time Warawa stopped, police officers stared at the stuffed rabbit in his hand. It made them all nervous. Why would a drug-addicted crook carry around a stuffed animal?

The police took Warawa down as he sat in the back seat of the taxi. Tactical officers set off an explosive flashbang outside the cab to distract him. A burst of light temporarily blinded Warawa as the windows shattered and shards sliced into his face. He screamed and clamped his hands over his eyes just as officers opened the doors and shoved him onto the street. Warawa resisted the handcuffs until an officer punched him in the torso.

Police found Warawa's loaded revolver inside a tear in the hide of the stuffed rabbit.

His short ride in the taxi would be Warawa's last moments of freedom before three years of trials that ended in a dangerous-offender designation and indefinite prison sentence.

* * *

News of Jose's horrific, random injury soon reached his family in Brazil. His younger brother, Ravi, told a Brazilian newspaper Jose lost an eye on that Circle Park bench and would lose the other in hospital. Still, Jose considered himself lucky. He'd survived a bullet to the head.

In the days after his injury, his family flew north from Fortaleza, in northeastern Brazil, to be at his bedside. Ten days after he was blinded, Jose left the hospital and held a press conference at Calgary's police headquarters with dark glasses covering half his face. Roberta sat beside him.

Jose still remembered the catastrophic moment. "I just heard something loud, felt something in my head."

Immediately he knew he was blind. He was certain of it.

Jose wasn't angry and showed no self-pity as the media crowded unseen in front of him.

"I could be in a graveyard right now," he said. "I can hug my parents. I can stay with everyone I love."

In the months ahead, Jose acquired the memorization and skill to navigate outside his front door each day. He walked with a cane, the days of soccer games and first attempts at Alberta snowboarding behind him.

Jose picked up the guitar again, an instrument he'd learned as a teenager, and played only by feel and sound. He learned Braille. Eventually, he received blue prosthetic eyes painted and modelled from his own in photographs.

In July 2010, Jose and Roberta married in Calgary.

"I don't know if you people are taking pictures or not," Jose said as he signed his marriage certificate, "but I'll smile anyway."

MODEL AIRPLANE GLUE

Rose Demuelenaere wasn't dumb. When a customer bought twenty-seven tubes of model glue in one week from the Ideal Grocery, he wasn't using it for airplanes. She'd refused to sell to him the last time he'd stumbled inside. Her suspicions were confirmed when the unkempt man became furious with her. He threatened her repeatedly and left in an angry haze.

"If you call the police, you're in trouble," the man bellowed on his way out the door.

Demuelenaere called the Calgary police. She'd never had a direct threat to report when she'd called them before. While she waited for an officer to arrive, she drew a sketch of the scruffy man who used her Ideal Grocery as a drug-sniffing supply outlet.

Constable Harvey Gregorash pulled up later that day, December 20, 1974, just after lunch. Demuelenaere told him the whole story.

Twenty-seven tubes of glue, she said.

Philipe Laurier Gagnon chose that inopportune moment to return to the store. That's him, Demuelenaere said with a pointed finger. Gagnon bolted out the door. Gregorash followed in his cruiser. The man wasn't hard to trail as he stumbled down the muddy alley.

Gregorash pulled up beside him and rolled down the window. "Would you like to get in the car? I'd like to talk to you about purchasing so much glue."

Gagnon's nose was a fiery, blotchy red, and a thick froth covered his lips. "No way am I getting into your police car. I'm going home."

Gagnon ran again and dashed between two homes decorated with Christmas lights. In the car, Gregorash lost sight of him, but people in the neighbourhood directed him to a garage on Ninth Street. It was a warm December day, and many people were in their yards. Some even hung laundry, five days before Christmas. They'd all seen Gagnon shamble past. They knew him. He introduced himself as Phil and said he'd moved to the Grandview neighbourhood so he could walk to his job at a poultry market.

Gagnon had lived in the garage for a month, though neighbours didn't know he'd arrived on the same day his parole expired. They didn't know he'd been released only months before from a three-year stint at Drumheller Institution for rape. No one guessed he was a glue addict or that he'd twice been involuntarily committed to the Alberta Hospital psychiatric facility. The neighbours barely noticed him. They definitely didn't know what the twenty-six-year-old had in his garage on the hill two blocks from Ideal Grocery.

The garage was locked when Gregorash knocked without receiving any answer. He called for backup. Constables Thomas Dick and Melville Linn arrived minutes later. The trio of officers looked for a way inside.

Dick found an open window and shouted inside. "Come on out, we want to talk to you."

"Come in and get me."

Dick and Gregorash climbed through the window into the darkness. The interior was converted into an apartment and partitioned into several small rooms. The two officers found a door and let Linn inside.

They found Gagnon in a tiny bedroom with a plastic bag pulled over his face as he inhaled the glue inside. There was a rifle in his other hand.

"Gun!" Linn yelled. The officers scattered.

Gagnon opened fire from ten feet away with a .22-calibre rifle.

Gregorash dropped behind a desk. "We just want to talk!"

Another shot roared. A bullet ricocheted off a desk and sliced a chunk from Gregorash's scalp above his right eye. The officers recognized a suicidal situation.

"Get the hell out," Dick ordered his fellow cops.

Gagnon shot Dick in the hip as he helped Gregorash escape. The bullet was stopped by the wallet in Dick's pocket.

The three officers ducked behind their cruisers and screamed into their radios. Gagnon locked the door behind them.

Officers and ambulances swarmed the neighbourhood. Police sped to the scene from all over Calgary whether they were ordered to or not.

"Get the hell back in the house and keep down," one officer yelled to neighbours who had come outside to investigate the commotion.

Police cordoned off the streets and evacuated those who weren't in a direct line of fire. Families scampered to safety behind rows of parked cars.

From inside the garage, Gagnon randomly fired through the walls at officers as they arrived. He had the .22-calibre gun and a powerful .30-06 rifle, both altered to fire automatically. The garage was stacked with boxes of ammunition. The gunshots echoed for miles.

One of the first officers on the scene was Detective Boyd Davidson. The forty-three-year-old was in the arson unit and only a few blocks away when the first shots were fired. The former football player and father of five was a popular officer. His colleagues knew how he'd pushed for an arson unit job after he worked a case with a fire marshall the year before. They'd also heard he visited the criminals he'd put in jail over a twenty-three-year career to help them adjust to life inside.

Davidson took cover with fellow officers beside a garage on the next property. Cops were pinned down everywhere the moment they stepped from their cars. The rare lull of bullets from the garage was always followed by another spray of shots. News reporters who wandered too close found themselves pressed against cars alongside the police.

Not all of Gagnon's shots missed. One officer was shot in the hand and another in the shoulder. Nobody wanted to poke their head out.

An officer took up a bullhorn. "Come on out, fella. You haven't got a chance."

"I'll get you bastards," Gagnon screamed back.

The owner of the garage lived nearby, and police told him to draw the interior. The picture was bad news. Five years before, the owner had dug a six-foot pit in a section of the floor where he intended to put a furnace. The furnace was never installed. To the officers, it was obvious where the gunman fired from. Worse, the garage walls were made of one-and-a-half-inch wood that stopped police bullets, but not those of the heaviest of the rifles Gagnon owned.

Another officer went to the ground with a bullet wound. Another shot tore into an officer's throat.

Paramedics rushed into the open to drag the wounded to safety. Officers provided a barrage of covering fire for the medics as they sprinted across sodden lawns. Ambulances constantly left the scene with patients and drove straight back when they were done. Emergency room staff at Calgary General gathered around a radio for news reports to anticipate casualties. They shouted questions at the paramedics who witnessed the ongoing shootout.

Officers continued to show up at the garage as word spread. More than half of the officers now in danger hadn't been ordered to respond. They carried rifles, shotguns, handguns, and shields. Officers peeked from behind light poles, trees, mailboxes, cars, garbage cans, and fences. An hour after he'd started shooting, Gagnon now held back more than a hundred police officers.

It was difficult for the officers, unable to move, to speak amongst themselves in the clatter of gunfire. No one knew exactly how many uniforms had shown up or where they were. There were too many targets.

Another officer bellowed in pain as he was hit.

Desperate, officers tried the bullhorn again. "Come on out, son. Come on out and you won't be hurt and you'll be out in time for Christmas."

"I got another of you fucking pigs!" Gagnon answered.

Officers decided to try tear gas. While that was prepared, Davidson used his shotgun to shoot out the windows of the next-door garage to lessen the chance of an officer being slashed by glass shrapnel from the sniper fire. Davidson then crouched to cover the officers picked to lob gas canisters through Gagnon's broken windows. The gunman's next shot burst through the walls of both garages and struck Davidson in the neck. A paramedic ran to his side as the detective crumpled to the ground.

The tear gas didn't work. The glue that lined Gagnon's nose weakened the impact of the toxic smoke, and he continued to shoot aimlessly.

After ninety minutes of gunfire, the police decided they needed something bigger. They made a phone call to Canadian Forces Base Calgary just before 3:30 p.m., and the military sent an armoured personnel carrier eleven minutes later.

The olive-green treaded carrier needed a convoy of police cars to make it through Calgary's afternoon traffic. The powerful vehicle drove to the edge of the yard with three soldiers from the Princess Patricia's Canadian Light Infantry inside.

"Hey army!" Gagnon greeted them gleefully. "Come on army!"

The soldiers discussed various ways to use the vehicle before deciding the direct route was best.

"It's the sledgehammer approach," Captain Merv McMurray of the Canadian Forces would later say. "It seems a bit of overkill."

Soldiers rammed the carrier into the side of the garage with a huge crash of sound. The garage door snapped, but did not give. The carrier backed up and took a second run. This time, it drove twenty feet inside. The soldiers backed up, again and again. The next two runs crumbled two of the garage walls. On the last run, they drove all the way through the garage. Large sections of wall hung off the carrier as it emerged on the other side.

In the ensuing quiet, Gagnon made a crouched, desperate run for the nearest house. There was a knapsack full of bullets on his back and a rifle in each hand. He fired one of them wildly.

"Come and get me!"

The officers opened up, destroying the blue house he was running to in a hailstorm of shots. Chunks of wood and broken glass flew into the air. Two hundred yards away at the roadblock, police and reporters dived for cover as bullets whined past them.

Gagnon was shot twenty-one times before he fell dead in the mud.

Edith Denniel watched the suicidal dash from across the street. Peering through her kitchen window the whole time, she described the standoff to a radio station over the phone.

"It sounded like a war movie," she said. "I could see at least eight officers waiting for him. He just came running out like there was a fire behind him."

Two hours after Gagnon and Gregorash met in the Ideal Grocery, it was all over.

Seven police officers were wounded. All survived but Davidson.

Ninety-eight officers had fired nearly five hundred rounds into the garage.

As the officers cleared out, Lieutenant Fred Parker reflected on the loss of his beefy, jovial partner. He and Davidson were partners in the arson unit and had known each other for years.

"All I can really tell you is that Santa Claus won't be around for Christmas," he told reporters. "The man with the heart of gold, gone."

DO NOT RESUSCITATE

On the morning of October 14, 1988, commissionaire Herbert Bushkowsky unlocked the heavy front doors of the Alberta Legislature and found a bearded man loading a .30-30 Winchester rifle on the stone steps outside.

"Do you have a problem?" Bushkowsky asked.

"Several," Robert Crawford replied.

Bushkowsky slammed the doors shut and ran to call 911.

Crawford was not in a good mood. The thirty-two-year-old had separated from his wife two years before, and she'd remarried the previous week. He'd been a schoolteacher in Calgary before his life fell apart in the wake of his divorce. He went to the legislature grounds in downtown Edmonton with a plan to make sure everyone knew how he'd been wronged in his divorce proceedings and subsequent custody dispute.

Crawford had lived in the town of Sylvan Lake with his brother Ken for several months. He tried to find work as a drywaller and promised to help build a new school gymnasium. The two had recently planned to build Crawford a new home, but the brothers hadn't seen each other in days.

Despite his attempts at a new life, it was obvious his previous one still bothered him.

Months before, the father of four had sent a letter to his ex-wife in Calgary that hinted at his plans for that chilly day.

"I shocked myself when I caught myself seriously planning a shootout with the police to make them kill me," he wrote.

A few days before his trip to the legislature, depressed and solemn, he'd visited his children in a Calgary park and given them gifts. He told his ex-wife he wanted to talk to her one last time. She thought it was a morbid joke.

Crawford came prepared. As Bushkowsky called police, the gunman taped a letter addressed to Alberta Social Services Minister Connie Osterman to the carved wooden doors, just above the brass handles.

"This last act is my armed revolt against all they do that's wrong," the note stated. "Here is for old Connie O., queen of poverty pimps. Her money-grubbing policies really make me sick. When marriages totter because of stress, she only adds on more, with threats and planned coercion like the pimps who attack the whore."

Crawford dropped a duffel bag on the wide steps with another note that listed his family members. "Police officers: This is a list of my next of kin if I die."

The note also said he declined any medical treatment he might need in the immediate future. For good measure, he taped two more notes, one to each arm, stating he refused all medical help. Paramedics would find those soon, Crawford thought.

He fired a single shot into the air as Edmonton Police Service officers arrived at the expansive provincial grounds. He wanted them to know he wasn't afraid to shoot. Officers scrambled to detour hundreds of government employees arriving to work through one of the many paths onto the grounds.

Crawford stalked his way around the grounds, prowling through the trees and bushes on the rolling land of one of the most visited spots in the capital.

He soon met Roy Brassard, a member of the Legislative Assembly from the central town of Olds. The gunman, with the rifle hidden behind his leg, ordered the politician to vacate the grounds. Brassard ignored him and returned to his car to fetch the office keys he'd forgotten.

Crawford waited for him until he came back to the main doors.

"I thought I told you to vacate the front of the building immediately."

"You're serious?" Brassard asked with wide eyes. He thought the guy was crazy. He hadn't seen the rifle.

"Yes," Crawford told him calmly. "I am."

Crawford spotted a police officer at the edge of the massive wading pool in front of the Legislature and headed straight for him. Constable Joe Pendleton warily backed away as the gunman aggressively moved in. The rifle wasn't pointed directly at the officer, but was close enough. Pendleton kept his gun holstered and yelled questions at Crawford, asking him if there was something wrong they could talk about.

Crawford didn't take the bait. "No, I don't think so. There's been enough talk already."

Pendleton ordered him to drop the rifle.

"Where's your backup?" Crawford asked. The more guns pointed at him, the better.

"There's police all over," Pendleton told him. "Just put the gun down."

Crawford considered the officer's demand and pointed the rifle at Pendleton's chest instead. "Are you ready?"

Pendleton abandoned his attempt at peace and dove for cover behind a hill. Crawford, disappointed he wasn't hit by the bullet he hoped for, walked away.

He slipped through one of the doors leading to the underground pedway near the construction of Edmonton's expanding subway line.

At the security desk inside the main doors, Bushkowsky stood helplessly as video cameras watched Crawford walk through the pedway toward the doors that led directly into the Legislature. There were no automatic locks to trigger from the security desk. He had a clear path. Inside, police officers stationed at the Legislature yelled at Bushkowsky to take cover behind one of the thick marble pillars in the rotunda.

As Crawford entered the building, security guard William Cockburn screamed at him to drop the rifle. Crawford turned and fired wide as Cockburn ducked into cover. He would later testify the gunman seemed to miss him on purpose before he continued further into the building. He aimed haphazardly and didn't seem intent on shooting anyone.

Two police officers waited for the gunman in the high-ceilinged rotunda and spotted him the moment he entered.

"Put the gun down. Do it now."

Again, Crawford opened fire instead. The officers found cover behind the marble lip of the wide fountain that welcomed visitors.

With no attempt to hide himself, Crawford turned and fixated on a third police officer behind him. Constable Mark Denouden stood behind the security desk with his revolver drawn. Crawford stalked toward him, and Denouden dropped to the floor just as another rifle shot echoed through the seventy-five-year-old halls. The bullet took an explosive chunk out of the desk, and wooden fragments carved into Denouden's right leg.

Behind Crawford, the other two officers decided he couldn't be reasoned with. They opened fire with seven shots. A bullet grazed Crawford's chest as he turned, and another destroyed one of his kidneys and severed his spine. He collapsed to the floor in slow motion, it seemed to the officers. They handcuffed him, though the rifle was now beyond his reach.

Denouden cradled the injured man's head in his lap as they waited for the ambulance.

"Why did you do this?" the officer asked as Crawford bled onto him. "We didn't want to do this."

Officers found four shells in Crawford's rifle. Three of them were blanks.

Days later, Crawford woke in a University of Alberta Hospital bed after emergency surgery, still in critical condition and paralyzed from the waist down. He was despondent that authorities ignored his notes refusing medical attention. A police officer stood by his bedside.

"I was counting on your guys' marksmanship to be a little better. Then I wouldn't be here," Crawford said.

He told the officer he'd do the same again if given a chance.

"You think about dying and wonder what's it's like. I felt the bullet hit me and then I went all numb. I felt myself falling over backwards and felt my eyes rolling back in my head. I told the paramedics to leave me alone. I didn't want their help. I should have been alive three hundred years ago in Japan. That's my style," Crawford said. "Some things are more important than life."

"You may think so," the officer said, "but I don't."

Weeks later, out of hospital, Crawford starved himself in his jail cell in another suicide attempt. He was sent to the Alberta Hospital for five weeks for psychiatric tests.

At trial, the judge didn't believe the depressed man meant to kill anyone, and he was acquitted on three counts of attempted murder. His four-year prison sentence was based on the rifle in his hand and the shots he'd deliberately fired wide.

Crawford watched his trial from a wheelchair in the prisoner's box.

FUEL FOR FIRE

In Nanton, the winter of 1907 was brutal.

Temperatures regularly fell to forty below zero in the village between Calgary and Lethbridge. Snow fell heavily and the wind blew strongly in the coldest winter even the oldest residents could remember. Families slept huddled against each other in layers of clothing and thick fur coats. The one-man RCMP detachment could hold no one in its tiny cell for fear they'd freeze to death.

As January turned to February, the cold brought desperation for Nanton's 380 residents and the dozens more on surrounding farms. The village was in its infancy and would not be officially incorporated as a town until later that year. It was isolated except for the four-year-old train track responsible for the village's existence.

The townspeople had nearly exhausted their supply of coal, and their fires burned low. There was little coal available because trains were slow on rails clogged with drifts of snow and ice. Although a nine-month strike at the Alberta Railway and Irrigation Company in Lethbridge had ended two months before, in December 1906, the resulting coal shortage was still severe across southern Alberta. To make matters worse, the village's population had grown and it now needed more coal than during the previous year's warmer winter. Residents had no choice but to wait for coal to come to them. The nearest mine was almost fifty kilometres away, and it was a dangerous trip over roads nearly impassable by horse and sled in the deep snow.

Some people split any expensive lumber they could find to feed their fires. Others tried to heat their homes with cheaper blacksmith coal, which was as about as effective as loading the coal into a shotgun and hunting a bear, wrote one resident in a letter to the *Nanton News* in early February.

"I think of the old scriptural saying 'Peace on Earth and goodwill toward men' and wonder if I will get sufficiently thawed out in time to go to church and thank Providence that I am still alive," read the letter printed on the front page.

"Of course we do not blame the government for the severity of the winter but the conditions for withstanding it could be greatly improved, without detracting from 'Sunny Alberta's' reputation of being the 'Banana Belt' of the North West we cannot blind ourselves to the fact that 'Jack Frost' does take undisputed sway for several months in the year, and this winter in particular. It has been prolonged almost to the limit of endurance."

The Alberta government should have ensured coal was properly distributed at a fair price, the letter read.

"If not willing to do so, there certainly should be a remedy and it will only be a matter of time before the people will demand it."

At the time, the weekly *Nanton News* was delayed for days because it was too cold to run a printing press. "Most of our readers will understand the situation and judge this issue of the *News* leniently," the paper read.

Hope came on the first of February, when merchant H. M. Shaw received word that the Lethbridge mine had sent a railcar of coal to Nanton on January 30, with plans to dispatch two more. Word spread quickly. By the next morning, forty teams of sleighs and wagons had arrived at Nanton's rail platform. They waited all day, huddled around frosted windows in anticipation as more farmers arrived for their share. The day passed with no train smoke on the horizon. Some farmers made the frigid trip back home for the night, while others stayed in the village. The next day was no better. No train, no coal. Fewer of the farmers bothered to go home. As the sun rose on the third morning, there were roughly 125 men watching the rail platform. The village burst with so many visitors, and the meagre coal that remained dwindled fast.

Later that day, a train finally came to Nanton, but continued north without unloading any coal. Hours later, a second train came through the snow. Again, it did not stop, and Nanton watched more coal pass them by for other customers. A third train did not come.

We should've just taken one of the first trains, some whispered to each other through chapped lips.

At 10:25 on the fourth morning, February 5, 1907, a third train filled with coal pulled into Nanton. The crowd was excited, but quickly despaired when a crew member explained none of the coal was destined for Nanton.

The town's only RCMP officer, Constable Thomas Currie, watched the crowd carefully as several men walked onto the tracks to block the train's progress. Locals told him the train should be held in Nanton by force until enough coal was unloaded.

Nonsense, Currie said. If several of us walk together to the nearest mine, we can survive the weather in numbers. No one agreed.

Station agent J. P. Longpre could feel the pressure. The leaders of the crowd wanted him to hand over three cars of coal. We'll just take it anyway, they told him. Longpre telegraphed the area superintendent for the Canadian Pacific Railway and told him residents of Nanton were blocking the track. The train carried seven cars of coal, Longpre said, all property of the CPR. Should he sell them the coal? What should he charge?

The response was decisive. Do not provide them with coal, read the telegraph response. Do not accept any money in what is clearly a highjacking. Demand that the RCMP protect the train and all its contents, it read.

Just as Longpre relayed his boss's demand that Currie protect the coal, the train began to pull out of the station and continue north. The crew had re-boarded, and smiled through the windows as they made their getaway. Several locals climbed aboard the train's back. Nanton resident Ira Shoop climbed over the caboose, ran the length of several cars, and dropped down behind the locomotive with Currie in pursuit. When the officer caught up, Shoop was trying to pull the train brakes. The officer drew his pistol and fired a warning shot. Shoop ignored the shot and the train squealed to a stop.

Currie arrested Shoop moments later. The officer led him off the train and released him immediately. There was nowhere to hold him with the RCMP detachment completely out of coal. It would be a frigid death sentence.

As the day wore on, the village took control of the coal shipment and moved it to a parallel track so a passenger train could pass. Residents walked the length of the train and disconnected each car from the next. They set the brakes faster than the crew could unset them.

"I don't see how two men are going to couple up these air tubes and throw off brakes as fast as two hundred can uncouple them and throw them on again," one of the train's brakemen said.

At noon, ninety minutes after the train reached Nanton, the crew left the platform to eat lunch. So did Currie.

The village residents stayed outside and held an orderly meeting on the platform to work out the details of their crime. Baptist minister J. S. Hunter stood on a three-foot box to chair the meeting.

The crowd decided to seize three of the seven coal cars and pay six dollars a tonne for what they stole. Farmers would get one tonne each while villagers would get half that. The Nanton schoolhouse would get two tonnes. Shaw was responsible for weighing the coal and ensuring it was divided equally among one hundred people who signed an agreement to pay their share of the eighty-six tonnes.

Through the afternoon, the coal was unloaded and distributed evenly among the villagers while the train crew watched helplessly. Currie did not intervene as he watched the men work. He didn't even try to send a message to his bosses. The next week, the *Nanton News* said the sole officer "held his nerve and courage."

By 5:00 p.m., the hijacking was complete and the train continued north more than six hours after it had arrived. It was a warmer night in Nanton.

The next day, Currie left town on business further north without filing a report of the robbery. His superiors learned of the incident when they were contacted by an angry CPR executive. At the CPR's request, an RCMP inspector investigated but decided no charges were warranted. The CPR did not push further. It would be unseemly to charge so many for acting on survival.

Shortly after, Currie was transferred to a post in Fort Macleod, eighty kilometres to the south.

An editorial in the *Nanton News* said the village residents did nothing wrong.

"The people of this vicinity feel that the course of the men who stopped the train was justifiable, under the circumstances. They have paid a big price for the coal delivered at Nanton and while their course may not have been in accordance with strict etiquette in high society, there was nothing sneaking, nor underhanded about it, and they have nothing to be ashamed of."

SOURCES AND REFERENCE MATERIAL

FORTY-FIVE HOURS–*Calgary Herald*; United Press International; Canadian Press; Calgary Police Service.

HEAVY METAL–*Edmonton Journal*; court transcripts and documents; reporter's notes.

CPR 63–*Windsor Daily Star*; *Regina Leader-Post*; Glenbow Museum; *Calgary Herald*; *Vancouver Sun*.

PUNKY–*Edmonton Journal*; *Edmonton Sun*; Canadian Broadcasting Corporation; CTV; court transcripts and documents.

THE KIDNAPPING OF HYMAN BELZBERG–*Calgary Herald*; Canadian Press; United Press International; Court transcripts and documents; *Fortune*; *Controlling Interest: Who Owns Canada* by Diane Francis (Seal Books, 1987).

"I WILL FIND YOU"–CTV; Canadian Broadcasting Corporation; court transcripts and documents; *Edmonton Journal*; reporter's notes.

HIRED MAN–*Calgary Daily Herald*; *Edmonton Journal*.

DAR–Court transcripts and documents; *Calgary Herald*; Canadian Broadcasting Corporation; *Lethbridge Herald*.

THE DOCTORS OF FAIRVIEW–Court transcripts and documents; *Edmonton Journal*.

PIPELINE–*Edmonton Journal*; Canadian Broadcasting Corporation; *The Globe and Mail*; Canadian Press; Court transcripts and documents; reporter's notes; *Saboteurs: Wiebo Ludwig's War Against Big Oil* by Andrew Nikiforuk (Macfarlane, Walter & Ross, 2002).

POLITICAL SUICIDE–*Calgary Herald*; *Lethbridge Herald*; Government of Alberta.

GUILTY CONSCIENCE–*Calgary Herald*; *Calgary Sun*: *CSI Alberta: The Secrets of Skulls and Skeletons* by Peter B. Smith (Heritage House Publishing Co., 2009).

HOCKEY BAG–Court transcripts and documents; *Edmonton Journal*; reporter's notes; CTV.

SNATCHED FROM SCHOOL–Court transcripts and documents; Canadian Press; *Edmonton Sun*; *Edmonton Journal*.

BURIED–*Calgary Herald*; Canadian Press; *Medicine Hat News*; *Lethbridge Herald*; *CSI Alberta - The Secrets of Skulls and Skeletons* by Peter B. Smith (Heritage House Publishing Co., 2009).

GREASE MONKEY–*Edmonton Journal*; *Regina Leader Post*; Canadian Press; *Calgary Herald*; *They Were Hanged* by Alan Hustak (Lorimer, 1987).

EIGHTY-EIGHT BULLETS–House of Commons committee transcripts; *Calgary Herald*; Canadian Broadcasting Corporation; *What Manner of Man: Darnell Bass and the Canadian Airborne Regiment* by James Ogle and Darnell Bass (General Store Publishing House, 1996).

THE PRETENDER–*Edmonton Journal*; court transcripts and documents; *The Devil's Cinema: The Untold Story Behind Mark Twitchell's Kill Room* by Steve Lillebuen (McClelland & Stewart, 2013).

CANNIBAL–*Manitoba (Winnipeg) Free Press*; *Edmonton Journal*; RCMP Veterans Association; *Swift Runner* by Colin A. Thomson (Detselig Enterprises, 1984).

NICK'S MILLIONS–Court transcripts and documents; Canadian Broadcasting Corporation; *Edmonton Journal*.

PRISONERS OF WAR–*Edmonton Journal*; Alberta Justice; *Calgary Herald*; *Montreal Gazette*.

MAYERTHORPE–Court transcripts and documents; *Edmonton Journal*; reporter's notes; Canadian Broadcasting Corporation.

HYPNOTIZED–*Calgary Daily Herald*; *Saskatoon Star-Phoenix*; *Edmonton Journal*; *Murder: Twelve True Stories of Homicide in Canada* by Edward Butts (Dundurn, 2011).

IN THE ROUGH–*Edmonton Journal*; Canadian Press; Edmonton Riverside Golf Club.

HOLLYWOOD SCRIPT–Court transcripts and documents; *Calgary Herald*; *Calgary Sun*; Canadian Broadcasting Corporation.

LESS THAN TWENTY DOLLARS OF GAS–Canadian Broadcasting Corporation; Canadian Press; Royal Canadian Mounted Police; *Calgary Sun*; *Calgary Herald*; Parole Board of Canada documents.

MOVING DAY—*Calgary Herald*; *Lethbridge Herald*; Calgary Police Service Interpretive Centre.

RUMOUR MILL—Court transcripts and documents; Canadian Press; *Edmonton Journal*; Canadian Broadcasting Corporation; *Stolen Life: The Journey of a Cree Woman* by Rudy Wiebe and Yvonne Johnson (Knopf Canada, 1998).

ROAD TO RUIN—Court transcripts and documents; *Edmonton Journal*.

SNOWMAN—Court transcripts and documents; reporter's notes; *Edmonton Journal*; Canadian Broadcasting Corporation.

LEMON AND GOLD—United Press International; *Calgary Herald*; Canadian Broadcasting Corporation; *Alberta Folklore Quarterly*; *Lethbridge Herald*; Glenbow Museum.

THE WORLD VERSUS PATRICK CLAYTON—Court transcripts and documents; *Edmonton Journal*; reporter's notes; Canadian Broadcasting Corporation.

GARRY BARRETT'S BITTER GRUDGE—*The Evening Journal* (Edmonton); *Calgary Daily Herald*; *Edmonton Journal*.

PARANOID—Court transcripts and documents; *Edmonton Journal*; *Edmonton Sun*; reporter's notes.

ART OF THE DEAL—*I'd Trade Him Again: On Gretzky, Politics and the Pursuit of the Perfect Deal* by Terry McConnell and J'Lyn Nye with Peter Pocklington (Fenn Publishing Company, 2009); Canadian Press; *Edmonton Journal*; court transcripts and documents.

LIKE FATHER, LIKE SON—*Edmonton Journal*; *Regina Leader-Post*; court transcripts and documents.

STRAY BULLET—Court transcripts and documents; *Calgary Herald*; Canadian Broadcasting Corporation.

MODEL AIRPLANE GLUE—*Calgary Herald*; Calgary Police Service; Canadian Press; *The Bruce Dubbin Memoirs* by Bruce Dubbin (Xlibris Corporation, 2011).

DO NOT RESUSCITATE—Canadian Press; *Edmonton Journal*; Government of Alberta

FUEL FOR FIRE—*Nanton News*; Canadian Broadcasting Corporation; "Vigilante Justice Tolerated: The Great Nanton Train Robbery, 1907" by William M. Baker, *Alberta History*, Winter 1997.

ABOUT THE AUTHOR

Ryan Cormier is a graduate of the University of Saskatchewan and of Carleton University's Master of Journalism program. He started as a reporter with the *Edmonton Journal* in 2003, and spent five years on the crime desk before going on field assignment in Afghanistan. He currently reports on court and legal affairs.